The European Institutions as an Interest Group

Interest Group

The Dynamics of Ever-Closer Union

The European Institutions as an Interest Group

The Dynamics of Ever-Closer Union

ROLAND VAUBEL

The Institute of Economic Affairs

First published in Great Britain in 2009 by
The Institute of Economic Affairs
2 Lord North Street
Westminster
London SW1P 3LB
in association with Profile Books Ltd

The mission of the Institute of Economic Affairs is to improve public understanding of the fundamental institutions of a free society, by analysing and expounding the role of markets in solving economic and social problems.

A CIP catalogue record for this book is available from the British Library.

ISBN 978 0 255 36634 2

Many IEA publications are translated into languages other than English or are reprinted. Permission to translate or to reprint should be sought from the Director General at the address above.

Typeset in Stone by MacGuru Ltd
info@macguru.org.uk

Printed and bound in Great Britain by Hobbs the Printers

CONTENTS

THE AUTHOR

Roland Vaubel is Professor of Economics at the University of Mannheim, Germany. He received a BA in Philosophy, Politics and Economics from the University of Oxford, an MA in economics from Columbia University, New York, and a doctorate in economics from the University of Kiel, Germany. He has been a researcher at the Institute of World Economics, University of Kiel, Professor of Monetary Economics at Erasmus University, Rotterdam, and Visiting Professor in International Economics at the University of Chicago (Graduate School of Business). He also worked with the European Commission as a *stagiaire* in 1973. He is a member of the Academic Advisory Councils of the German Ministry of Economics and Technology and the Institute of Economic Affairs and an associate editor of the new journal *Review of International Organisations*.

Professor Vaubel specialises in international finance, international organisations, public choice and social policy. He has been editor of *The Political Economy of International Organisations* (with T. D. Willett), *Political Competition, Innovation and Growth* (with P. Bernholz and M. E. Streit) and *Political Competition and Economic Regulation* (with P. Bernholz). The IEA published his Hobart Paper *The Centralisation of Western Europe* in 1995 and his Wincott Memorial Lecture *Choice in European Monetary Union* in 1979.

FOREWORD

The main thesis of Roland Vaubel's monograph is unfortunately about to be proved resoundingly right. The EU bureaucracy has for many years strived to 'streamline' the cumbersome decision-making process by which 'Europe' inches its way 'forward' to 'ever closer union' or, as Professor Vaubel would put it, to 'ever greater centralisation'. The Treaty of Maastricht, the creation of the euro and the Treaty of Nice were all strongly opposed by public opinion in many countries, but were all adopted in the end. The Constitutional Treaty is simply the latest instalment in this series. Now renamed less pretentiously as the Treaty of Lisbon (itself a shorthand), it will probably soon be ratified by all 27 members of the Union. Sheer perseverance on the part of the European bureaucracy, active support or passive consent on the part of governments, rational ignorance on the part of the public – who, for the most part, are not consulted – are all that is needed.

Yet the Constitutional Treaty was rejected via referenda by French and Dutch voters in May and June 2005. Two years later it reappeared in diminished length, but no less dangerous substance, as the Lisbon Treaty, only to be rejected again, this time by Irish voters in June 2008. One might have thought that the Eurocracy would have had the decency to shelve the project. Not a bit of it. It has been reworked to accommodate Irish objections (abortion, taxation, neutrality), pacify the Poles and the

Czechs, and even address concerns of the acceding Croatians. The Irish will be asked to vote again shortly (opinion polls are enthusiastically in favour) and the last serious obstacle will be removed in May 2009 when the German Constitutional Court will confirm – barring a judicial tsunami – the constitutionality of the Treaty.

Anybody wondering what this means for our future as European citizens would do well to read this monograph. Future generations will be amazed at the ease with which free and democratic peoples were deprived of their liberty. How did it come to be that freedoms built up over centuries were brushed aside in just a few years? The short answer is that most people were not consulted on the matter, and when they were, they objected – but then were bought out. For the most part, their democratically elected governments gave up their freedoms for them, knowing full well that if put to a vote, the whole project would fail. The craven attitude of the British government, first promising a referendum on the ratification of the Constitutional Treaty, then withdrawing its promise in the case of the reworked (but basically similar) Lisbon Treaty, is a case in point.

Professor Vaubel applies public choice analysis to the issue, showing how all the power brokers in the story have an interest in European centralisation, including member governments. He points out, with devastating logic and many amazing examples, just how Europeans are being deprived of their democratic rights on a massive scale, as the EU continues its uninterrupted marathon race towards 'ever closer union'.

What is the answer to the problem? Read on, dear reader. Although Vaubel is too insightful an observer to offer you much hope, he shows that just a few small constitutional amendments are needed to halt the process of European centralisation and restore democratic rights to their proper owners. What is needed is a grassroots revolt against the hijacking of our rights, to which Vaubel's detailed academic research is an essential contribution.

VICTORIA CURZON PRICE

Geneva

March 2009

The views expressed in this monograph are, as in all IEA publications, those of the author and not those of the Institute (which has no corporate view), its managing trustees, Academic Advisory Council Members or senior staff.

SUMMARY

- The creeping centralisation of political power at the European level has been due to institutional deficiencies rather than economic or social needs. It cannot adequately be explained by 'functionalist' theories but can be explained by political economy.
- The European institutions (Commission, Parliament, Court and Council) share a vested interest in ever-closer union because this enhances their power and prestige.
- There is also a self-selection bias: 'euromantics' are more prone to working for the EU than 'eurocritics'.
- Evidence from various sources reveals that, in EU affairs, the preferences of top Commission officials and Euro-parliamentarians diverge widely from the preferences of the citizens. The national parliamentarians and the media are shown to be biased in favour of EU centralisation as well, though to a lesser degree.
- It follows that popular referenda will have to play an important role in EU decision-making. For example, they ought to be obligatory for all Treaty amendments, but each member state may decide whether they shall be binding.
- The Lisbon Treaty, by lowering the majority requirements in the Council, by transferring more competencies to the EU and by dramatically extending the general empowering clause,

would strongly reinforce the centralising dynamic. It would not enable the national parliaments to control EU legislation.

- The main activity of the European institutions is regulation. Since the transition to majority voting in 1987, for example, more than fifty EU labour regulations have been introduced. They have not been a response to competitive deregulation at the national level but the deliberate strategy of a majority of member states to impose their high levels of regulation on the more liberal minority.

- The fact that the Commission has executive, legislative and quasi-judicial powers is incompatible with the classical principle of the separation of powers. The Commission ought to become an ordinary civil service subordinated to the Council. After-tax salaries at the Commission are shown to be out of control.

- The European Parliament lacks many characteristics of a normal parliament. A second chamber ought to be added which includes representatives of the national parliaments determined by lot and which shall have no other power than to block centralising legislation.

- The European Court of Justice, like most constitutional courts, has been a motor of centralisation. Very few of its members have had judicial experience in their home country. A second court ought to be added which includes delegates from the highest national courts and which shall exclusively decide cases potentially involving the distribution of competencies between the Union and the member states.

TABLES

The European Institutions as an Interest Group

The Dynamics of Ever-Closer Union

1 INTRODUCTION: THE DRIVING FORCES OF THE CENTRALISING DYNAMIC

Since Britain joined the European Community, the activities of European institutions have expanded at a very rapid pace. From the first half of the 1970s to the second half of the 1990s, the total number of legal acts more than quadrupled.[1] The number of directives increased from 22 per annum in the early seventies to 98 in 2006. Over the same period, the budget of the European institutions has more than doubled relative to the GDP of all member states. And from 1968 to 2006 the number of staff increased by 85 per cent relative to population. The total number of EU officials now exceeds 40,000. Moreover, there are large complementary bureaucracies occupied with EU affairs in the member states. According to a recent estimate, their size is about two-thirds of the European bureaucracy (Haller, 2008: 162–8).

All this reflects a spectacular process of political centralisation – more dramatic than anything we have witnessed in peacetime so far. What explains the seemingly inexorable dynamic?

Jean Monnet, the father of the European Economic Community, correctly predicted the self-propelling growth of the

---

1   Alesina et al. (2005: Table 3). The peak was in the second half of the 1980s. This is confirmed by another study (König et al., 2006: Figure 1) which, however, uses a much narrower definition (excluding all acts that have subsequently been repealed) and does not start before 1984. From 1971–75 to the peak in 1986–90, Alesina et al. report an almost fivefold increase, whereas, over the whole period, the number of acts rose by a factor of 4.4.

European institutions. But he did so for the wrong reasons. He believed that European integration in specific sectors such as coal and steel would produce 'spillovers' into other sectors which would then require further 'harmonisation' or centralisation in still other sectors, and so on. This process would lead to 'ever-closer union', as stipulated in the preamble of the EEC Treaty and now in Article 1 of the Treaty on European Union (TEU).

As a matter of fact, there are hardly any examples of this type of dynamic. The creation of the European Economic Community in 1957 – Monnet's *pièce de résistance* – was not needed to prop up the European Coal and Steel Community.[2] Even the European Atomic Energy Community was not a spillover from coal but a technological and highly political project. Nor was it the case that the removal of distortions in one sector led to the removal of distortions in other sectors, as economists trained in the theory of the second best may suspect. The centralising dynamic cannot be accounted for by 'functionalist' theories. As I shall try to show, it has to be explained by political economy or, more precisely, public choice theory. It is driven by the self-interested activities of the main institutional actors.

This is not to deny that the various stages of the process were interconnected. The first connection was simply the 'community method', which, once accepted and practised, could be applied to ever more fields. The cost of learning the method had to be borne only once – after that it was 'sunk'.

Moreover, one step triggered the next because the existence and growth of international organisations alter the political equilibrium. As soon as a new organisation sees the light of the day, it

---

2   For the historical analysis see Gillingham (2003).

struggles to secure its survival and growth. Political and economic events that previously would have been inconsequential are now exploited by the newborn organisation to obtain more staff, more funding and more competencies. Its growth enables the organisation to increase its power even more when the next disturbance arrives, and so on. Alternatively, if the shock reduces the demand for its services, the institution will use its accumulated power to resist the required rollback. Thus, in the long run, international organisations grow even if the demand for their services merely fluctuates around a constant mean. Their tasks expand. They gradually ratchet upward. It is much more difficult to close an international organisation than to found it. International organisations may lose their function and change their name but they hardly ever die.[3]

Finally, the centralising dynamic is self-propelling because agreement often requires 'side payments'. Whenever a new piece of legislation is considered, some member states tend to assert, rightly or wrongly, that they would be harmed and need to be compensated. One form of compensation is the addition of new competencies for the international organisation which especially benefit such veto players. I will give a few examples of such expansive issue linkages.

First, when the EEC was founded in 1957, the French government claimed that the customs union would benefit Germany rather than France and that, as compensation, the subsidy of agriculture and development aid should be shared to the benefit

---

3   The Bank for International Settlements, the OEEC (now OECD), the International Bank for Reconstruction and Development and the International Monetary Fund (since the collapse of the Bretton Woods system) are probably the most telling examples.

of France. Moreover, the French government insisted on atomic energy cooperation and a Community competence in the field of 'social regulation' because France had the most restrictive labour regulations. The main beneficiaries of the customs union were, however, the small and central member states (the Benelux countries), and France shared in the gains from trade as well. But the French government got its way.

Another example is provided by the UK. After Britain had joined the Community as a major net contributor in 1973, the Labour government elected in 1974 renegotiated the terms of accession and insisted on the creation of a European Fund for Regional Development which would spend large sums of money in the UK. When its request was granted, it called a referendum about whether the UK ought to stay in the Community. In 1975 the referendum supported membership and the Fund was established.

Again, when the Single European Act was adopted in 1986, the 'poor four' of the time (Spain, Portugal, Greece and Ireland) made their assent conditional on a doubling in real terms of the structural funds. They succeeded. Similarly, when the European Economic Area was established and the Treaty of Maastricht was negotiated, they obtained a 'Cohesion Fund', which would subsidise specific projects in their countries.

There seems to be only one example of a veto player not bought off by additional Community expenditure: the Thatcher government negotiating the British rebate in Fontainebleau in 1984.

Sometimes the package also included non-Community bilateral issues. The Maastricht Treaty, for example, was triggered by German unification, which required the assent of the former allied powers. There is abundant evidence that the French president, François Mitterrand, demanded agreement on European monetary union in exchange.[4] The Social Agreement of Maastricht, promoted by France as well, was also part of the deal. The British government did not want to get involved in these projects and opted out.

To some extent the centralising dynamic, i.e. political integration, is also driven by market integration, even though these two types of integration are completely different processes. The common market was a highly successful attempt to remove the barriers to trade and capital movements that the national governments had erected. It increased efficiency as well as freedom. Moreover, by strengthening competition, it reduced the need for government intervention in the economy. Political integration or centralisation, by contrast, is a threat to liberty. The more we centralise, the more powerful the state as a whole becomes. In a centralised state, be it national or supranational, the citizens' cost of exit is high and the scope for comparisons is restricted.

Even though political integration and market integration are entirely different and in some respects opposites, market integration promotes political integration in two ways. First, trade liberalisation requires some procedure for the settlement of disputes. If an executive body such as the European Commission is appointed guardian of the treaty, there is always a danger that it will be given additional powers which it will use to expand its sphere of influence. If arbitration is left to a court or a panel of experts, these judges have a vested interest in conferring more powers on the

4   See Teltschik (1991: 61); Attali (1995: 313ff); Favier and Martin-Roland (1996: 202); Dyson and Featherstone (1999: 364); Quatremer and Klau (1999: 170ff); Vaubel (2002: 460–70).

common executive because, by doing so, they increase their own scope of jurisdiction. Moreover, the judges will take their decisions by majority vote. This enables the majority of member states to raise their rivals' costs by imposing their own restrictive regulations on the minority. The European Union is a case in point, as Chapter 4 will show.

The second channel from market integration to political integration is less well known. Once international trade and capital movements have been liberalised, they are highly responsive to all sorts of disturbances, notably government interventions. Any increase of taxes or regulations by one government would cause large capital outflows and a severe loss of competitiveness. Market integration puts the participating national governments under intense competitive pressure. It increases the incentives for them to 'harmonise' or even centralise taxation and regulation at the international level. Market integration may therefore drive national governments into the hands of the international institutions. This is why the international executive, parliament and court have strong incentives to promote market integration, which in due course will increase their scope.

By now market integration in the European Union has almost been completed. What remains on the agenda of the European institutions is political integration, which is simply another word for centralisation. Without fundamental reform of EU institutions, their quest for ever-closer political union cannot be stopped.

Moreover, just as exit, or the threat of it, can restrain a government from taxing and regulating its citizens too heavily, secession, or the threat of it, can put a limit on centralisation. The best example is Canada. In no other country of the world is the share of central government expenditure in total government expenditure as low as in Canada (amounting to 45.8 per cent), and it keeps falling (Vaubel 2009: Table A.1). Before 1948, this was largely due to the fact that Canada did not have a constitutional court. Constitutional matters were decided by the Privy Council in London, which was not interested in centralising Canada. Since then, however, the most important cause of decentralisation in Canada has been Quebec and its threat of secession. Can Britain become the Quebec of Europe?

The following sections examine each of the European institutions separately. I show why and how they are pressing for centralisation and examine what can be done against it. I then ask whether the Treaty of Lisbon solves any of these problems or whether it actually makes them worse. Finally, I discuss alternatives to the centralising institutional framework and explain how the process of reform might be initiated.

2 THE EUROPEAN COMMISSION

The European Commission is not only, not even primarily, the guardian of the treaties. It has many functions. It implements legislation, spends money, conducts quasi-judicial proceedings as part of its competition policy and so-called 'anti-dumping' policy, and it has the sole right to initiate EU legislation. This combination of executive, legislative and judicial functions is inconsistent with the principle of the separation of powers. Indeed, it is a dangerous agglomeration of powers.

The most striking anomaly is the Commission's monopoly of legislative initiative. Without a proposal from the Commission, no legislation is possible. The Commission is the legislative agenda-setter or gatekeeper of the Union. Since the Treaty of Maastricht, it is true, the European Parliament and the Council may formally request the Commission to propose legislation on a certain subject. But the Commission has been quick to point out that it does not feel bound by such requests (Commission Report SEC (95) 731, p. 14). More recently, the Commission reasserted its right as follows: 'By virtue of the Treaties, the Commission has a virtual monopoly on exercising legislative initiative within areas of Community competence' (COM (2002) 278 final, p. 5). Moreover, since Council and Parliament had always been free to communicate their wishes to the Commission, the right to request a proposal made no difference at all. It was designed to mislead, not to solve the problem. The Treaty of Lisbon does not even address the issue.

The Commissioners are chosen by the governments, confirmed by the European Parliament and appointed by the European Council. They decide behind closed doors and, if necessary, by simple majority. Their voting record is not published. Thus, all EU legislation has to be proposed by a body that is neither elected by a parliament nor accountable to the public.

Once the Commission has made a proposal, the Council and the European Parliament may amend it. The majority requirement in the Council depends, however, on the vote of the Commission. If the Council agrees with the Commission, it can adopt the act by qualified majority; if it does not, unanimity is required (Article 250–252 TEC). Thus, the Commission interferes with the legislative process even after it has made a proposal. Under the co-decision procedure (Article 251 TEC), any amendment would also require the assent of the European Parliament, which shares the Commission's vested interest in European centralisation. In any case, the Commission will not submit a draft legislative act that it expects to be altered against its wishes. Thus, it cannot come as a surprise that EU legislation is a one-way street in the direction of ever more centralisation. The member states may stop and park but they cannot turn back. Even if some Union policy fails dismally, the Commission cannot be stopped by ordinary legislation. This is the above-mentioned ratchet effect. It is called '*acquis communautaire*'.

The Commission's monopoly of initiative may have been justified in earlier times when the focus was on market integration because the Commission was less likely to relapse into protectionism than the Council. But the common market is now virtually completed and firmly entrenched. The Commission's agenda is therefore political unification and preservation of the centralist *acquis*. Here the Commission's monopoly turns out to be highly problematic. It ought to be abolished – at the very least for all legislation that does not reverse the liberalisation of markets.

Quasi-judicial functions

The Commission also possesses quasi-judicial functions. First, its Directorate General 'Competition' conducts investigations against firms suspected of collusion or abuse of dominant market power. The Commission may search their offices, seize documents, pass a verdict and impose (huge) penalties. The ultimate decision does not rest with the Director General or the Commissioner in charge of the Directorate but with the full college of the Commissioners, most of whom are political figures and have no expertise in competition policy – let alone the specific case at hand. Obviously, such judicial decisions ought to be taken by an independent court or authority or by a commission of experts, as is the case in most industrial countries.

Another example of quasi-judicial proceedings is anti-dumping policy. It is of a similar nature except that it is usually abused for protectionist purposes. Once again, the Commission investigates the case, passes a verdict and proposes a duty or minimum price on the foreign exporter. Anti-dumping measures may be justified if a foreign exporter who is temporarily selling below cost gains a dominant market share in the importing country (so-called predatory dumping). Examples are very hard to come by but it is a theoretical possibility. The argument presupposes that the foreign exporter has acquired, and is abusing, a dominant market position as defined by competition policy. The Commission does not, however, apply the criteria of dominant market power and abuse of such power (which it is using in competition policy) to its anti-dumping policy. Ideally, anti-dumping policy ought to be transferred to the independent competition authority or be abolished altogether.

Third, in its role of guardian of the treaties, the Commission acts as a public prosecutor. Once more, it is doubtful whether the college of Commissioners possesses the required expertise and legitimacy. Ideally, a separate and independent European public prosecutor should take the member states to court if they violate their obligations. He or she ought to be appointed by those who have ratified the treaties: the parliaments of the member states.

If the Commission were stripped of its legislative and quasi-judicial functions, it would become a genuine civil service, the non-elected branch of a European executive. But how well does it perform as a civil service?

The Commission as a civil service

The European Commission is a rare case of an *independent* civil service. It is not a secretariat taking orders from governments or parliaments. According to the treaties, 'the members of the Commission shall, in the general interest of the Community, be completely independent in the performance of their duties. In the performance of these duties, they shall neither seek nor take instructions from any government or from any other body' (Article 213 TEC). Legally, the Commission is subject to the juris-diction of the European Court of Justice, but the court almost always sides with the Commission because it shares its vested interest in centralisation. Moreover, the Commission may be dismissed by the European Parliament acting by a majority of two-thirds but, as I shall show, the parliament, too, favours centralisation.[1]

Is there anything the governments or parliaments of the member states can do against the centralist bias of the Commission?

First, they may amend the Treaty. But this requires unanimity. As long as one government or parliament – say, Belgium – protects the Commission, the latter can do what it wants. Second, every five years the governments and parliaments of the member states may cut the Commission's budget in the multi-annual financial framework. But such a cut would also require unanimity. If the member states cannot agree, the budget stays constant in real terms.[2] Any single government can, however, veto a real increase. Third, if a Commissioner wishes to be reappointed, the government of the country may threaten to withhold its support. But many Commissioners prefer to retire anyhow.

Even if the Commission were not granted independent status by the treaties, democratic control would be weak because international organisations are far removed from the attention of voters. The chain of delegation from the citizens to international institutions is extremely long. As a result, the international agents may not do what their principals, the citizens, want them to do. There are two major reasons for this 'principal-agent problem'.

---

1   As Haller (2008: 92f) reports from his interviews, 'none of the interviewed MEPs saw any serious problem in the relations with the Commission'. Here are some of his quotes: 'There are conflicts [in the EP] but not with the Commission ... The Commission is a daughter of the parliament ... One does not hurt each other'.

2   If the member states cannot agree on the financial framework, a complex procedure is set in motion but the status quo is the fallback position.

The principal-agent problem

First, centralisation, especially at the international level, raises the voters' cost of political information. Partly, this is due to sheer distance: for most citizens, the seat of the international organisation is much farther away than the national capital. The international organisation uses foreign languages that the majority of voters do not understand. The well educated do not mind or may even enjoy listening to foreign languages, but others feel excluded. The cost of information also rises because the centralisation of ever more policies prevents the citizens from comparing the performance of public institutions in different countries ('yardstick competition'). Finally, decision-making at the international level is opaque because the issues are complex and abstract and the decisions are taken behind closed doors.

Second, quite apart from the *cost* of information, the citizens lack a sufficient *incentive* to take up and use the available information about EU policymaking. The citizens' access to decision-makers is more restricted, the weight of each vote is smaller, and the individual share in the savings to be reaped from cost-cutting measures is lower than at the national or local level.

High costs and weak incentives explain the voters' 'rational ignorance' in matters of EU policy. Their ignorance relates to the Commission as well. In 2004, for example, people were asked in an EU-wide survey whether the headquarters of the European Commission are in Strasbourg. Only 22 per cent of the respondents knew that this is not the case (Eurobarometer 61).

People also feel powerless. As another survey (Table 1) shows, 40 per cent of respondents expressed the opinion that they have no influence at all on EU decisions – compared with 29.2 per cent concerning their home governments; 28.8 per cent believe that they have some or a great deal of influence on their home government but only 19.5 per cent say this for the European Union.

Table 1 **Question: How much influence, if any, do you think the opinion of people like yourself has on the decisions taken by …**

	a) the government of your country?	b) the institutions of the European Union?
No answer	0.2	0.3
A great deal	5.4	3.9
Some influence	23.4	15.6
Not much influence	38.1	34.4
No influence at all	29.2	40.0
Don't know	3.6	5.5
Total	100.0	100.0
Number of answers:	17,298	

Source: Eurobarometer, 44.1, Nov./Dec. 1995, Question 73

In another poll, 76 per cent of the respondents agreed that citizens have too little influence in EU affairs (Haller, 2008: Figure 4.1). In a very recent survey, 56 per cent took the view that 'the EU does not represent ordinary people'.[3]

Is there also evidence that the Commission is not behaving the way the citizens want it to?

The best I can offer is a survey comparing attitudes towards the EU among the general public on the one hand and among 50 top civil servants at the Commission and 203 Europarliamentarians on the other hand (Table 2).

---

3   Open Europe, Poll on the future of Europe, 2007.

Table 2 **EU-related opinions of the general public, 50 top Commission officials and 203 members of the European Parliament in nine EU member states (per cent)**

	General public	Top Commission officials and Euro-parliamentarians
The European Union should strengthen its military power in order to play a larger role in the world:		
agree strongly	16	31
agree somewhat	30	34
disagree somewhat	30	17
disagree strongly	21	15
don't know	3	2
The European Union should have its own foreign minister, even if my country may not always agree with the positions taken:		
agree strongly	21	54
agree somewhat	44	24
disagree somewhat	18	6
disagree strongly	12	15
don't know	5	1
Generally speaking, do you think that Turkey's membership of the European Union would be:		
a good thing	21	44
a bad thing	32	33
neither good nor bad	40	19
don't know	6	4

Source: European Elite Survey, Centre for the Study of Political Change, University of Siena, May–July 2006 (as published by Roper Center for Public Opinion Research MCMISC 2006-Elite) and Transatlantic Trends 2006, Topline Data, June 2006.

As can be seen, the share of those who are strongly in favour of strengthening EU military power, appointing an EU foreign

Table 3 Net salaries at the European Commission and in the central governments of selected member states

EU grade		Commission		EIB	Germany	UK	France	Denmark	Italy
		Non-expatriate	Expatriate						
A4/A5 (eg Counsellor)	S	100	123	147	63	74	81	60	27
	M	100	121	149	62	61	80	53	24
B4/B5 (eg Secretary)	S	100	120	151	70	84	59	66	41
	M	100	119	158	67	67	53	59	43
C4/C5 (eg Security officer)	S	100	120	147	71	57	57	62	46
	M	100	117	154	67	44	50	53	37
Average	S	100	121	148	68	72	66	63	38
	M	100	119	154	65	57	61	55	35
	M+S	100	120	151	67	65	63	59	36

Source: European Commission, Comparative Study of the Remuneration of Officials of the European Institutions, June 2000.

minister and admitting Turkey into the EU is about twice as large among the top Commission officials and Euro-parliamentarians as among the general public.

Does the Commission act 'in the general interest of the Community' and 'perform their duties' as the above quotation from the treaties suggests? The most visible sign of a serious principal-agent problem is the extraordinary level of after-tax salaries.

Table 3 presents the most recent evidence. It is based on a comparative study of net remunerations compiled by the Commission. The after-tax salary of a non-expatriate EU official (for example, a Belgian working in the Commission in Brussels) is set equal to 100 to facilitate comparisons. I have selected three grades (A4/A5, B4/B5 and C4/C5) for which data from all five reference countries and the European Investment Bank (EIB) are available. The first line (S) refers to a single person, the second (M) to a married couple with two children. The overall average for all five member states is 58 per cent of the EU after-tax salary, i.e. on average a non-expatriate Commission official earns 72 per cent more than a comparable national civil servant. The expatriates get 20 per cent on top. Of course, the salary differential is much larger for nationals from low-income countries. For eastern Europeans these salaries must be like a dream. The study also shows that salaries are higher at the Commission than at the NATO Secretariat or UN agencies in Brussels. Salaries at the European Investment Bank are about 50 per cent higher than at the Commission. The usual justification one hears is that the EIB has to be competitive vis-à-vis private banks. But most members of its management committee, including the chairman, a former politician, do not have any banking experience.

There have been some valiant attempts to address the salary

problem. In 1984, both chambers of parliament in Germany asked the federal government to use its influence in the Council and curb the salary hikes at the Commission. The German government replied that the Commission's monopoly of initiative was 'an unsurmountable obstacle'. When in 1991 the Council found a way to resist the Commission, the civil servants at the Commission went on strike. The compromise that was finally reached made hardly any difference.

Third, an independent bureaucracy, especially if it is international, is likely to suffer from financial negligence and corruption. Fisman and Gatti (2002), for example, find a significantly positive correlation between political centralisation and corruption. A Eurobarometer poll in January 2004 revealed that almost two in three EU residents believe that fraud against the EU budget is common, and only one in five says that EU institutions are effective in fighting it. In another survey in the same year, 74 per cent agreed with the statement that 'clientelism and corruption are problems in the political institutions of the EU in Brussels' (Haller, 2008: 345).

The European Court of Auditors has refused to clear the Commission's accounts each year since 1994. In 1998, the auditors estimated that about half the accounts of the Commission's programmes were incorrect. In its report for 2006, the Court found that €15 billion or 30 per cent of the agricultural funds were not subject to proper checks and that €3.8 billion or 12 per cent of the structural funds had been paid out in error. It also criticised 'a lack of evidence to support the calculation of overheads or the staff costs involved'. It concluded: 'Errors of legality and regularity still persist in the majority of EU expenditure due to weaknesses in internal control systems both at the Commission and in Member States ... Regardless of the method of implementation applied, the Commission bears the ultimate responsibility for the legality and regularity of the transactions underlying the accounts.' The report for 2007 highlighted unacceptable spending errors in all but two of the seven policy areas. At least 11 per cent of cohesion spending was found to be erroneous.

In 1999, the whole college of Commissioners resigned because an independent committee of inquiry had found evidence of widespread fraud, corruption, mismanagement and nepotism. For instance, the French Commissioner Edith Cresson had employed her dentist and friend as a scientific adviser; the Portuguese Commissioner João de Deus Pinheiro had hired his wife as a national expert; and the wife of Spanish Commissioner Manuel Marin had also been given a high-level job. In 2002, the Commission's chief accountant (Marta Andreasen) was suspended (and later sacked) after she refused to sign accounts she believed were unreliable (her office had uncovered numerous cases of possible fraud). In 2003, the French director of the European Statistical Office was involved in a corruption scandal and had to resign. The European anti-fraud office has estimated the damage from fraud at €1,500 million in 2004. There are similar problems in other international organisations.[4]

The alliance with special-interest groups

Many critics claim that the Commission is particularly accessible to the demands of special-interest groups. There are several reasons why this is likely to be true.

---

4   A recent and well-known case was the United Nations oil for food programme in Iraq. In 2005, an independent commission of inquiry chaired by Paul Volcker revealed serious fraud and corruption in its administration.

The college of Commissioners is a small body, and it is less costly for lobbyists to win over a majority in a group of 27 than in a parliament of 782 deputies. The Commission is also an easier target than the Council because it decides by simple majority, whereas most Council decisions require a qualified majority of 73.9 per cent or even unanimity.

Moreover, bureaucrats do not need to be re-elected. Politicians are more cautious in dealing with special-interest groups because such favours may cost them votes among the majority of voters. The bureaucrats of the Commission are not restrained by the prospect of elections.

Of course, if voters face high costs of information and have hardly any incentives to get informed, lobbyists have a field day. Special-interest groups seek to attain political outcomes that democracy alone would not bring about. The lobbyist and the median voter are rivals. European political centralisation, by aggravating the rational ignorance of voters, magnifies the influence of organised interest groups. Euro-corporatism affects all EU institutions but especially the Commission.

What do the lobbyists try to obtain from the Commission? They want to influence the legislative proposals but these may be amended by the Council and the Parliament. What the Commission can supply on its own is money, administrative regulations and information about lobbying opportunities in the Council and the Parliament. Money may go to the members of the interest group or to the special interest organisation itself. In 2005–07, the European Commission gave more than €50 million to dozens of non-governmental organisations, including the European Trade Union Confederation (€4.8 million) and the International Lesbian and Gay Association (€1.5 million).

With regard to administrative regulations, there are more than a hundred consultative committees in which representatives of interest groups advise the Commission and the Council (Falke, 1996: 132). The treaties do not provide for this 'comitology' but the European Court of Justice approved it in 1970.

The Commission supports special-interest groups because bureaucrats and lobbyists have common aims. Both are interested in political centralisation because it helps them to escape the attention of voters. The Commission and the interest groups form an alliance against the median voter – against democratic control.

Andersen and Eliassen (1991) have compared the influence of pressure groups at the European level and in the member states. They came to the conclusion that 'the EC system is now more lobbying oriented than in any national European system' (p. 178).

There are many symptoms. The first is the highly protectionist EU trade policy ('fortress Europe'), notably with regard to agriculture, textiles, shoes and steel. Second, more than one half of the budget is devoted to organised interest groups, especially agriculture. Third, more than three-quarters of the pages of the EC official *Journal* cover special-interest legislation (Peirce, 1991: Table 2). Fourth, there is a committee of interest-group representatives, the Economic and Social Committee (ECOSOC), which has to be consulted on all pertinent legislation. Its members receive compensation from the EC budget. ECOSOC employs more than five hundred persons, half of them translators, who are also paid by the European Union. Fifth, there are at least fifteen thousand private lobbyists trying to influence the European Union institutions in Brussels. The total number of EU lobbyists, including those from other governmental and non-governmental organisations, is estimated at 55,000 (*European Voice*, 2004). There is even an institute specialising in the training of EU lobbyists ('L'Institut Européen des Affaires Publiques et du Lobbying').

Euro-corporatism has come as a surprise to those who believed with James Madison that centralisation would weaken the power of pressure groups because the various local or regional interests would neutralise each other. What Madison did not foresee was that the more encompassing interests would combine at the higher level of government and that they would increase their influence because centralisation raises the information costs and lowers the information incentives of the citizens. The historical experience of the United States and the European Union has exposed Madison's fallacy.

Reforming the Commission

The institutional mechanics contrast starkly with the 'euromantic' visions of people at the Commission. Many 'eurocrats' are highly motivated and dedicated to their cause. Lofty ideals – such as peace, international cooperation and solidarity – tend to play a more prominent role in the Commission than in a national civil service. At least that was my impression when I worked there. The principal-agent problem is, however, much more serious at the international level. In the end, civil servants from so many countries and diverse backgrounds are primarily united by the collective bureaucratic interest of their organisation. There is not much else they can agree on.

Two types of reform seem to be necessary.

The Commission ought to be stripped of its non-executive functions. Too many powers are concentrated in the hands of a single institution. The Commission should give up its monopoly on, indeed its right to, legislative initiative. It must not determine the legislative majority requirements in the Council. It should not have to be consulted about pending legislation at all. Competition policy ought to be delegated to an independent competition authority. The same is true for anti-dumping policy, if it is to be kept at all. A European public prosecutor should replace the Commission as guardian of the treaties. These reforms would diffuse power and permit specialisation. They follow from the classical-liberal principle of the separation of powers.

As the non-elected branch of a European executive, the Commission also ought to become an ordinary civil service.[5] Each Commissioner should be subordinated to a minister elected by a parliament. The Commissioners would become state secretaries.

Who would be the ministers? The Commissioners ought to receive their instructions from those who have appointed them: the members of the Council. Each Council of Ministers would elect one of its members as EU minister for its affairs (and another member as deputy). Each EU minister would at the same time be responsible for the corresponding ministry in his or her home country. This is how the Presidency of the Council has worked in the past. But it is not necessary that all councils of ministers are chaired by ministers from the same member state. The Council has experience in supervising civil servants who execute EU policies. For example, in the field of foreign and security policy, the Council appoints a 'High Representative' of the European Union who is subordinate to the presidency (Article 18 TEU). He serves at the same time as the Council's secretary-general.

In the past, the presidency has rotated among the member

---

5   This is also the conception of the European Constitutional Group (2007) to which I owe, and with which I share, more ideas than I can acknowledge.

states every half year. The Lisbon Treaty would extend the term of the presidency to two and a half years. As German history shows, however, such a dual ministerial role may last much longer. When the Kaiserreich was founded in 1871, Otto von Bismarck served as Chancellor of Germany and prime minister of Prussia at the same time up to his dismissal in 1890. When he embarked on his social insurance legislation in 1880, he also took over the Prussian board of trade. The dual-role model is perfectly feasible and highly effective.

In an ordinary national civil service, there is no need for a collective body comprising the state secretaries of all ministries. Hence, the college of Commissioners might be dissolved.

These changes in the administration of the European Union may seem revolutionary if compared with the status quo. But they merely reflect the normal role that a civil service plays in a classical liberal democracy. A civil service must not have other than executive functions and it should not be independent.

There is more room for doubt as to who ought to supervise it. Why should the European civil service not be subordinated to ministers elected by the European Parliament? Why should the college of Commissioners not become a cabinet of ministers, the government of the Union, as many seem to think?

3 THE EUROPEAN PARLIAMENT

The European Parliament is not as representative as one might wish or expect. It is less representative of the wishes of citizens than the national parliaments. Table 4 reveals the problem. The survey data are from the 1990s because such questions are rarely posed. In particular, they are not asked by Eurobarometer, which is sponsored by the European Commission.[1]

Table 4 **Preferred levels of decision-making for the three most important issues in ten EU member states (percentages based on responses)**

Preferred governmental level	Mass public	Members of national parliaments	Members of European Parliament
Regional	12	7	3
National	45	48	43
European	42	44	54

Sources: Schmitt and Thomassen (1999), European Representation Study, Table 3.1.

The members of the European Parliament, the national parliamentarians and the citizens were asked which level of decision-making they preferred for various policy fields: European, national or regional. Schmitt and Thomassen (1999) report the

---

1   For a harsh critique of Eurobarometer, see Haller (2008: 259–61).

percentages of the respondents for the three issues that were considered most important. Decision-making at the European level is preferred by 54 per cent (a majority) of the members of the European Parliament but by only 42 per cent (a minority) of the citizens. The national parliamentarians (44 per cent) are much closer to the citizens than to the European parliamentarians, but they are also biased towards centralisation. This evidence suggests that the European Parliament is not at all representative of the preferences of citizens regarding European political integration. The national parliamentarians are much more representative in these matters, but since they are biased as well, the decision about the distribution of competencies between the EU and the member states ought to be left to the people themselves – in referenda.

It is also interesting that the national parliamentarians are biased in favour of *national* decision-making and against *regional* decision-making. Each group of parliamentarians prefer their own level of decision-making. This may be because politicians try to be elected to the parliament they prefer. Ardent Europhiles are more likely to run for the European Parliament than stubborn Eurosceptics. This is the self-selection bias.

Furthermore, once politicians have been elected to a parliament, they possess a vested interest in expanding the powers of their parliament. The more competencies are transferred to the European Union, the more rewarding is the life of a Euro-parliamentarian.

In the same survey, people were asked whether they were 'proud to be Europeans'. The distortion was very similar: while 55 per cent of citizens said 'yes', the share was much higher among members of the European Parliament (75 per cent) and the national parliaments (68 per cent) (Schmitt and Thomassen, 1999: Table 2.2).

The most visible sign of the European Parliament's centralist bias is the fact that it invariably demands a larger European Union budget than the member states have proposed. Within the member states, by contrast, parliaments typically try to cut the spending proposals of the executive. In view of these biases, the European Parliament should not be responsible for decisions affecting the division of labour between the Union and the member states. For example, it should not elect the ministers supervising the Union's civil service. Nor should it be in charge of such EU legislation. Before discussing the alternatives, I shall give a more complete account of why the European Parliament is not an ordinary parliament.

Not an ordinary parliament

One important reason is the cartel among the three main party groupings: the Social Democrats, the People's Party (mainly Christian Democrats) and the Liberal Party. They share the parliamentary posts on a rotating basis, and they vote in common much more often than the parties in a national parliament tend to do. At the national level, one typically observes a large opposition party that is excluded from power. Indeed, political theory predicts that, in a normal parliament, parties form a '*minimum* (contingent) winning coalition' because they do not want to share power unnecessarily. The European Parliament is different. As there is no European government to be elected by a minimum winning coalition, there is little from which the majority may wish to exclude the minority. There is no game to win. Moreover, owing to self-selection and a vested interest in centralisation, the Euro-parliamentarians of most parties share a common bias. Rather than compete, they form one large party: the party of EU centralisation. The European Parliament represents itself.

Moreover, the fundamental democratic principle that each vote must have the same weight does not hold in elections to the European Parliament. As is well known, each member state receives a predetermined number of seats, and the country weights differ considerably from the population weights and the share of voters. The smaller member states are entitled to a disproportionately large share of the seats. For example, just to mention the most extreme distortions, a vote in Luxembourg or Malta counts nine times more than a vote in Britain, France, Italy, Germany, Poland or Spain. The Treaty of Lisbon does not remove the disproportionality but increases it.

The European Parliament is also too large. It is probably by far the largest parliament in the world. With the accession of Bulgaria and Romania in 2007, the number of seats rose to 782. Several intergovernmental conferences tried to reduce the number of seats but, as was to be expected, the Euro-parliamentarians themselves resist any major cut. The new parliament elected in 2009 will have 751 members, a reduction of less than 4 per cent. It is true that the number of parliamentarians should increase with the number of voters to be represented. But there is a limit to what can be handled efficiently. A huge parliament like this is not only excessively costly; more importantly, it weakens the individual member's incentive to be well informed. The case for representative democracy rests on the argument that a deputy has a stronger incentive to be informed than a voter. Thus, in EU affairs, the case for representative democracy is weaker, and the case for referenda is stronger, than in national politics. There is also evidence that large parliaments are more interventionist because each parliamentarian wants to be rapporteur on some issue. In a very large parliament, each member deals with some minor issue and is busy inventing very detailed regulations.[2]

Furthermore, citizens are badly informed about the European Parliament. In an opinion poll after the European elections of 2004, people were asked whether the statement that 'the next elections to the European Parliament will take place in June 2006' was true or false. Only 29 per cent of the respondents recognised that the statement was false (Eurobarometer 61, 2004).

Citizens not only know very little about the European Parliament, they also care very little. Voter participation is very low and continually falling. In the European elections of 2004, average voter turnout was 45.7 per cent, even though voting is compulsory in four member states. In ten member states, turnout even fell short of 40 per cent. It is much lower at European elections than at national elections. In Germany, for example, voter turnout at the European election was 43 per cent compared with 77.7 per cent at the national election one year later. To some extent, low turnout is a sign of opposition: analysis of the referenda on EU issues reveals that the share of the no-votes rises with voter participation (Haller, 2008: 14ff).

The Euro-parliamentarians themselves care very little as well. Whoever has visited a typical plenary session knows that attendance is poor. The most recent case study reveals that, in the second half of the 1990s, 34 per cent of the parliamentarians were absent when votes were taken compared with less than 10 per cent

---

2   See the interviews with Euro-parliamentarians in ibid.: 92.

in the Belgian parliament (Noury and Roland, 2002: Table 6). The European Parliamentarians also tend to represent interest groups rather than the electorate at large. Sixty-six per cent have been or are functionaries of interest-group organisations (Haller, 2008: Table 3.4). In 2005, 2,030 such organisations were accredited with the European Parliament.

Even the administration of the Parliament would appear to be flawed. For example, it has two headquarters, one in Strasbourg and one in Brussels, plus a General Secretariat in Luxembourg. The parliamentarians, their staff, their documents, etc., are constantly on the move, and there is duplication. This is costly. Strasbourg is far from the Union's centre of power – it is not where the action is. The headquarters in Strasbourg are the most visible sign that the Parliament is not at the heart of Europe.

Finally, the European Parliament does not have the usual powers of a parliament. It is probably the only parliament in the world that does not have the right to propose legislation. Moreover, it has no say over the Community's revenue or its 'compulsory' expenditure. The approximation of tax rates is also beyond its control. This enables the governments of the member states to evade parliamentary control with regard to taxation by jointly setting minimum tax rates at the European level. EU law obliges the national parliaments to 'implement' such tax increases. Thus, parliaments have lost one of their foremost rights – the right to control taxation.

All these anomalies indicate that the European Parliament is not an ordinary parliament. It provides the trappings of a democratic structure but it is really more like an appendix. Moreover, it is biased towards political centralisation at the EU level.

Citizens are aware of the democratic deficit. In a Eurobarometer survey of 2006, people were asked whether they were satisfied with democracy in the EU and in their own country.[3] The overall share was 50 per cent for the EU but 56 per cent for the member states. The difference in favour of democracy at home exceeded ten percentage points in Finland (36), Austria (30), Sweden (29), Denmark (28), the UK (20), Luxembourg (20), the Netherlands (18) and Germany (12). But in Portugal, Italy and all new member states except Cyprus respondents expressed a preference for the EU. The survey also reports people's perception of political corruption in their country. The lower the corruption, the higher is the preference for democracy at the national level. The correlation coefficient (r) is equal to minus 0.91. That is an almost perfect negative correlation.

Reforming the European Parliament

The European Parliament ought to be reformed in three ways.

First of all, the Parliament ought to conform to democratic principles. Second, its costs must be controlled. Third, the European Parliamentarians must not be entitled to legislate on the division of labour between the Union and the member states. Issues of subsidiarity are better decided by members of the national parliaments or citizens themselves.

In a union of 27 member states, it would be too cumbersome to involve all national parliaments in ordinary EU legislation. It is enough that they or their citizens decide about the ratification of treaty amendments. A second chamber comprising delegates of the national parliaments ought, however, to be added to the

3   Eurobarometer 65 (Spring 2006). The survey includes Croatia and Turkey.

European Parliament. This is how the members of the European Parliament were recruited until 1979, when direct election was introduced. The second chamber would be responsible for all legislation potentially affecting the role of the member states, and it would decide whether there is such an effect. Draft legislative acts not taken up by the second chamber would go to the first chamber. Both chambers and the Council would have the right to propose legislation.

The national parliamentarians in the second chamber would lack a vested interest in centralisation at the EU level. Being members of their national parliaments at the same time, they would not gain power by legislating in favour of the European Union. Nor would they be biased in favour of national legislation. There may still be a self-selection problem, however: parliamentarians who adore the European Union are more likely to specialise in EU affairs and to aim at being sent to the second European chamber. To avoid such self-selection, the delegates ought to be chosen by lot in each parliamentary group. Selection by lot is a good old constitutional practice going back to the republics of ancient Athens and medieval Venice.

The first and the second chamber should be entirely separate. They should not collude. Ideally, they should assemble in different places. The first chamber could be located in Brussels and the second in Strasbourg.

We have seen above that, in EU matters, the national parliamentarians think more like citizens than the Euro-parliamentarians do. But they still have some pro-EU bias. This is shown not only by opinion polls but also by many referenda. In ten instances, voters have rejected the European policy proposed by their government and the majority in their parliament:

in Norway, 1972 (accession to the EEC), in Switzerland, 1992 (accession to the EEA), in Norway, 1994 (accession to the EC), in Denmark, 1992 (against the Maastricht Treaty), in Denmark, 2000 (against joining the eurozone), in Ireland, 2001 (against the Nice Treaty), in Sweden, 2003 (against joining the eurozone), in France, 2005 (against the constitution), in the Netherlands, 2005 (against the constitution) and in Ireland, 2008 (against the Lisbon Treaty). But even in those cases in which the voters concurred, the electoral majority was almost always much lower than the parliamentary majority. Table 5 presents the evidence.

Table 5 **A comparison of national referenda and parliamentary votes on issues of EU policy (per cent)**

Country	Year	Issue	Yes to referendum	Yes in parliamentary vote
Austria	1994	Accession to EU	66.6	80.0
Finland	1994	Accession to EU	56.9	77.0
Sweden	1994	Accession to EU	52.7	88.0
Malta	2003	Accession to EU	53.6	58.6
Slovenia	2003/04	Accession to EU	89.6	100.0
Hungary	2003	Accession to EU	83.8	100.0
Slovakia	2003	Accession to EU	92.5	92.1
Estonia	2003/04	Accession to EU	66.8	100.0
Spain	2005	EU constitution	76.2	92.4 (Parl.) 97.4 (Senate)
Luxembourg	2005	EU constitution	56.5	100.0 (June) 98.2 (Oct.)

Source: Haller (2008: Tables 1.1, 1.2a and 1.2b).

How can the Euro-centrist bias of the national parliamentarians be explained?

The typical member of a national parliament faces a dilemma. On the one hand, he or she wants to be re-elected. On the other hand, he or she would like to be promoted by the cabinet and to the cabinet. The members of the cabinet, however, as we shall see in the next chapter, have a vested interest in joint decision-making at the EU level in several respects.

If, in some policy fields, parliaments do not represent the wishes of the citizens, then the citizens themselves should decide in popular referenda.[4] That is the Swiss system. It can be confined to those policy areas in which, for obvious reasons, the citizens and the members of parliament tend to have very different interests. I shall return to this problem.

---

4   Weiler (1999: 350f) proposes a procedure for legislative initiatives and for legislative ballots at the time of the European parliamentary elections.

4 THE COUNCIL – THE GOVERNMENTS OF THE MEMBER STATES

The members of the Council, i.e. the ministers of the member states, including the prime ministers or their equivalents, have been elected by their national parliaments. But they have a stronger interest in European centralisation than their back-benchers do because they possess direct legislative power at the EU level. They also differ from ordinary parliamentarians, however, because they wield executive power at the national level. This explains why the members of the Council are more willing to transfer legislative powers, and less willing to transfer executive powers, to the European Union. To a large extent, the European Union enables the national ministers to gain legislative power at the expense of their fellow parliamentarians. The European Union disempowers the parliaments of the member states.

At the European level, each minister has to share legislative power with the ministers of other member states, the Commission and the European Parliament. But EU decision-making provides an additional option for political action. The risk of losing power is small as long as the Council has to agree unanimously and the powers are shared by the EU and the member states. There is merely the risk that the majority of the judges at the European Court of Justice may interpret EU legislation in an unexpected way. Thus, it is relatively easy to explain why, in the first three decades of its existence, under the unanimity rule, the European

(Economic) Community was very attractive to the executives of all member states and why the Union was given shared rather than exclusive powers.

Membership in an international organisation is attractive for the national ministers and civil servants because it provides opportunities for travel, media attention and job placement. The EU Council is essentially a club of ministers and state secretaries, membership conferring various amenities and prestige, especially on the representatives of small or poorer countries. Moreover, since the Council is a club of incumbents, they share the desire to be re-elected. Hence, they are likely to support each other, especially before elections, giving praise or even money from the structural funds.[1] Even if, from an ideological point of view, the government of one country prefers the opposition in another country, it is the government of the other country which has most to offer. If all member governments act in unison, they are less likely to be criticised by the opposition and the media at home.

The ministers also share the problem that they depend on the support of some well-organised interest groups (farmers, declining industries, trade unions, etc.). Catering for interest groups is not popular with the electorate at large. Politicians are tempted to hide such 'dirty work' by delegating it to an international organisation. The Common Agricultural Policy, the 'Anti-Dumping' Policy and the plethora of EU labour market regulations are cases in point. The ministers share these electoral aims with the national parliamentarians backing them.

The ministers have an incentive to engage in log-rolling at the

---

1 Research on this point seems to be lacking for the European Union, but Dreher and Vaubel (2004) show that the subsidised credits of the International Monetary Fund are significantly larger before elections in the recipient countries.

expense of third parties. For example, they tend to give away the powers of lower-level governments and of independent public institutions (the judiciary, an independent central bank, competition commission, etc.) if they can obtain something else in exchange.

For individual ministers, decision-making in the Council may be a way of evading cabinet discipline and parliamentary control at home. Even if the legislation requires the assent of the European Parliament, it is easier to get it passed at the EU level than by each national parliament separately because the overall majority in the European Parliament does not have to be composed in a specific way.

Finally, the ministers of the member states and their parliamentary majorities at home are interested in EU-wide tax and regulatory cartels. With regard to collusive taxation, the VAT Directive of 1992 is the most telling example. The German government, which lacked a domestic parliamentary majority to raise its VAT rate, got its way by proposing a European minimum rate that was higher than the prevailing German rate. The European minimum tax rate exceeded the prior VAT rates of three member states. It raised the average VAT rate in the Union and it was designed to do so. There are also several labour market regulations that had to be adopted unanimously, for example the directives on collective redundancies (1975), employees' rights in the event of transfers of business (1977) and equal treatment of men and women (1975, 1976, 1979), as well as eleven directives on health and safety adopted prior to the Single European Act (1987). These were instances of regulatory collusion.

To my knowledge, there exists no survey that directly compares the attitudes of Council members and ordinary citizens.

But much of the work of the Council is influenced and carried out by the civil servants of the member states. Table 6 compares the views of these civil servants and the general public.

Table 6 **EU-related opinions of the general public and top decision-makers among national civil servants, parliamentarians and journalists (per cent)***

Issue	General public	National civil servants	Parliament-arians	Media leaders
Support for EU membership	48	96	92	91
Benefits from EU membership	43	92	90	86
Strengthening the European Parliament	60	68	70	73

* Sample size: 3.778 persons in EU-15
Source: EOS Gallup Europe, *The European Union: A View from the Top*, Special Study, 1996

The gap between citizens and civil servants is huge. While only a minority of the electorate favours EU membership, support among civil servants is overwhelming. The same is true for the question whether, on balance, the country benefits from EU membership. The difference is much smaller with regard to the role of the European Parliament. Civil servants are not enthusiastic about parliamentary control. The next column ('parliamentarians') is more difficult to interpret because it includes national and European parliamentarians. But it confirms the result of Table 4 that both are more EU-minded than citizens. Except on the issue of whether the European Parliament ought to be strengthened, national civil servants are even more biased towards EU decision-making than politicians. The last column confirms the impression that media leaders, including those in television and radio, share the opinions of the politicians on whom many of them depend.

From collusion to raising rivals' costs

Unanimity has gradually given way to qualified majority voting in the Single European Act and the treaties of Maastricht, Amsterdam and Nice. If individual ministers run the risk of being outvoted in the Council, they are less eager to grant powers to the European Union. They have to balance the gains from winning against the losses from being outvoted. Apparently, from 1986 onwards, all governments believed that on balance they would benefit by accepting qualified majority voting. What made them change their mind?

Globalisation is a possible explanation. As was mentioned above, the liberalisation of trade and capital movements in Europe and globally has put the tax and regulatory policies of the individual governments under intense competitive pressure. Any national government raising taxes or regulations unilaterally would be punished by large capital outflows. Tax revenue, real wages and employment would decline. If all European governments raise taxes or regulations, the penalty imposed by the market is much lower. Some have even predicted that market integration would reduce national taxes and regulations and trigger a race to the bottom. These predictions are clearly exaggerated, both theoretically and empirically.[2] Nevertheless, the

2   Mobile capital and labour will be attracted not only by low taxes but also by an optimal provision of public goods, notably infrastructure. Moreover, game theory suggests that the race is not to the bottom but to the 'Nash point', i.e. the point at which no participant can benefit by changing their strategy while the other players keep theirs unchanged. While it is true that corporate tax rates have declined

governments' acceptance of more majority voting in the Council may have been a response to competitive deregulation at the national level.

In a recent article (Vaubel, 2008), I have shown that this hypothesis has to be rejected with regard to labour markets. Employment protection in the member states did not decrease prior to the Single European Act of 1986. There was a minute decline from 1986 to 1991, but even then labour market regulation was at a historically high level in all member states except Spain. Thus, the transition to more majority voting in the Single European Act (1986) and the Social Agreement of Maastricht (1991) was not a reaction to competitive national deregulation.

The Social Agreement was a pet project of French president Mitterrand and Commission president Jacques Delors, both socialists. After the fall of the Berlin Wall, as was mentioned above, Chancellor Kohl of Germany needed Mitterrand's assent to German unification. Even though Kohl's Christian–liberal coalition had dismantled labour regulations in the 1980s and was clearly opposed to re-regulation, the German government accepted the Social Agreement just as they were willing to trade in the autonomy of the Bundesbank (which they did not control anyway). The political leaders of France – not only the socialists – had demanded 'social union' and monetary union for decades, and this was their window of opportunity. The Conservative British government was not interested in either part of the deal and opted out.

Since 1991, a clear tendency towards labour market deregulation has been visible in the member states (ibid.). To some extent,

since the first half of the 1980s in Europe and elsewhere, revenue from these taxes as a share of GDP or of total tax revenue has generally increased in the EU-15.

this may have been due to the liberalisation of EU capital movements introduced in 1989 and again in 1991 as part of the Maastricht Treaty. Thus, even though the national deregulation of labour markets did not precede EU labour market regulation, it may have been expected by the politicians who agreed to majority voting in the Social Agreement.

The transition to qualified majority voting with regard to the 'health and safety of workers' (in the Single European Act) as well as 'working conditions', 'information and consultation of workers', etc. (in the Social Agreement) had far-reaching consequences. Since 1989, the EU has introduced at least 58 directives regulating the labour market. Moreover, the Council has approved at least ten EU-wide labour market agreements between employers and unions, thereby rendering them universally binding.

Majority voting enables the interest groups and governments of the highly regulated member states to extend their own regulations to the other member states. Economists call this 'the strategy of raising rivals' costs'. It is well known from the history of federal states like the USA and Germany.[3] It has recently been shown to apply to the International Labour Organisation as well.[4] The common level of regulation imposed on the minority is higher than the level originally prevailing in the decisive member state because the latter is no longer subject to the competitive pressure from low regulation in the minority of member states. This may explain why the EU workplace regulations have tended to be even more restrictive than the previously existing national

3 For a survey, see Vaubel (2004). More recent case studies are published in Bernholz and Vaubel (2007).

4 For the econometric evidence, see Boockmann and Vaubel (2009).

regulations of the most restrictive member states.[5] But this finding is consistent with collusion as well.

The voting record of the Council, which has been published since 1993, reports unanimous agreement on most labour market directives. Yet there is broad agreement in the literature that very many of them would not have been adopted unanimously if unanimity had been required.[6] If the minority is too small to block the legislation, it usually votes with the majority. Why does the minority rarely record its dissent? There are several reasons.

First, governments that are opposed to a regulation, but lack a blocking minority, may nevertheless accept it because, if they did not, they would be excluded from the negotiation of the details.

Second, they may not want to annoy the majority because they would be punished in future legislation. The majority is especially likely to be annoyed if the voting record is published. The governments constituting the majority prefer a record reporting unanimity or at least a large majority because none of them wants to be seen as decisive, i.e. as responsible for shifting the balance in favour of regulation. This is especially true if the regulation is sought by an interest group rather than by a majority of voters.

Third, any government voting against a labour regulation adopted by the majority on the Council is highly vulnerable to criticism from opposition parties at home. It bears the burden of

---

5   For some evidence, see O'Reilly et al. (1996).

6   For instance, Mattila (2004: 31) in his well-known analysis of Council voting notes that 'the observed number of contested decisions is really a downward biased estimate of the true amount of dissent [because] Council members do not necessarily want to record their dissent officially'. Similarly, Hagemann and DeClerk-Sachsse (2007: 20) call open opposition 'the tip of the iceberg in terms of how much disagreement over proposals is actually present in Council negotiations'.

proving that the overwhelming majority of the other politicians in the Council was wrong.

Thus, the strategy of raising rivals' costs is consistent with a record of unanimity. It does not require that the Council actually decides by majority but merely that it would have been entitled to do so. If the decisions of the Council are not contested, however, we do not know whether they are due to regulatory collusion or the strategy of raising rivals' costs. That is why, in the following, I shall focus on those regulations which are known to have been contested in the final vote or challenged during the negotiations.

EU regulation of labour and financial markets

Since 1993, the following EU labour regulations have been openly contested in the final vote:

- the Working Time Directive (1993);
- the Directive on Safety and Health Requirements for Work on Board Fishing Vessels (1993);
- the European Works Council Directive (1994);
- the Directive on Safety and Health Requirements for the Use of Work Equipment (1995).

In all four cases, the UK was among the contestants. In one instance, the Working Time Directive, the British government was the only contestant. It abstained even though it was opposed to the measure. It then challenged the directive at the European Court of Justice on the grounds that health and safety at work were not the primary concern of this directive and that, therefore, it had to be adopted unanimously. The Court sided with the legal services of the Commission and the majority of the Council.

The EU regulation was more restrictive than prior UK legislation in all four instances. For example, working time in the UK exceeds the EU average. A significant part of the British workforce works longer than 48 hours, the limit that is to be finally imposed. For the EU as a whole this share is very small. As Table 7 shows, the UK has the least restrictive labour market regulations in the EU-15 (excluding Luxembourg, for which there are no data). It is followed by Denmark and Ireland. These three countries are most likely to suffer from the lowering of the upper majority requirement that the Treaty of Lisbon holds in store. This may be one of the reasons why the Treaty was rejected by the Irish in their referendum.

Many more directives have been disputed in the Council. Seven, all requiring no more than a qualified majority, were classified as 'B-points' by the Commission, which means that they were considered controversial. In three further instances, newspaper or research reports indicate that the directives were challenged during the negotiations:

- the Equal Treatment Directive (2000);
- the Directive on Informing and Consulting Employees (2002); and
- the Temporary Workers Directive (2008).

In all three cases, the UK, Ireland and Germany were among the objectors. The first two directives were also criticised by the Danish government. But the Danes and Germans soon backed down.

Table 7 Indices of labour market regulation, EU-15 excluding Luxembourg,[a] 1990s

	Council votes	OECD[b]	Botero et al.[c]	Gwartney and Lawson[d]	Nickell and Nunziata[e]	Average rank
UK	10	0.9(1)	1.02(3)	6.6(2)	0.35(1)	1.75
Denmark	3	1.5(3)	0.95(2)	7.6(1)	0.94(3)	2.25
Ireland	3	1.1(2)	1.04(4)	4.9(3)	0.52(2)	2.75
Austria	4	2.3(6)	0.80(1)	4.2(4)	1.30(5.5)	4.13
Finland	3	2.1(4)	1.73(10)	3.4(6.5)	1.15(4)	6.13
Netherlands	5	2.2(5)	1.68(9)	3.1(11)	1.30(5.5)	7.63
France	10	2.8(10)	1.59(8)	3.4(6.5)	1.39(7.5)	8.00
Sweden	4	2.6(8.5)	1.05(5)	3.3(9)	1.58(10)	8.13
Belgium	5	2.5(7)	1.77(11)	3.6(8)	1.39(7.5)	8.38
Germany	10	2.6(8.5)	1.57(7)	3.2(10)	1.54(9)	8.63
Greece	5	3.5(13)	1.89(12)	4.0(5)	n.a.	10.00
Italy	10	3.4(12)	1.51(6)	2.4(13)	1.92(12)	10.75
Spain	8	3.1(11)	2.18(13)	3.0(12)	1.62(11)	11.75
Portugal	5	3.7(14)	2.36(14)	2.1(14)	1.93(13)	13.75

Notes: Ranks in parentheses

a Luxembourg has two votes in the Council.   b Weighted index for 1990s, from 1 (minimal regulation) to 4 (maximal).
c Employment laws index for 1997, from 0 (minimal regulation) to 3 (maximum).   d flexibility in hiring and firing (= sub-index 5Bii),
average of 1990, 1995 and 2000, from 0 (minimal flexibility) to 10 (maximum).   e employment protection 1986–95, from 0 (no
protection) to 2 (maximum).

For seven years the Commission's proposal of the Temporary Workers Directive was warded off by a blocking minority. When the Union was enlarged in May 2004, the Polish government joined the blocking coalition. After the change of government in Poland in the autumn of 2007, however, Poland changed sides, the minority lost their veto power, and the directive was adopted in 2008. The government of Gordon Brown chose to assent in the Council in exchange for some face-saving temporary concessions on working time. These have been blocked, however, by the European Parliament.

There is also a directive that was consistently fought by all Conservative British governments but immediately accepted by the new Labour government in 1997. That is the Part-Time Directive. The minimalist British implementation of the directive, however, reveals a lack of enthusiasm.

Thus, even though in 1997 the Blair government had accepted the Social Agreement of Maastricht and with it all EU regulations that the others had introduced on this basis in the meantime, Labour got into trouble over EU labour regulation as well. Unlike its Conservative predecessor, however, it always voted for those EU labour regulations which it could not stop, and it never went to Court.

In a way, the Conservatives' decision in 1991 not to veto the Social Agreement but to demand an opt-out may be interpreted as an attempt to raise rivals' costs as well. If the others adopted new EU labour regulations, acting unanimously or by qualified majority, the UK would gain a competitive advantage with regard to labour costs. As was to be expected, however, this advantage was short-lived. If the Major government had vetoed the Social Agreement in 1991, the latter would probably never have been

adopted. By 1997, the window of opportunity that German unification had opened for French EU policy in 1989–91 had closed,
and the Christian–liberal German government would not have
accepted the Social Agreement as part of the Amsterdam Treaty.
Would a British veto have deprived John Major of his election
victory in 1992?

The example shows that 'opt-outs' for particular member
states and 'enhanced cooperation' among subgroups of member
states are not as harmless as many people think. Even if the
unwilling are not included for the time being, the others may
form a regulatory or tax cartel, and some future government may
decide to join it irreversibly.

The strategy of raising rivals' costs by EU regulation has not
been confined to the labour market. Another example is the
Financial Services Directive (2003), which was rejected in the final
vote by the UK, Ireland, Luxembourg, Sweden and Finland, even
though they could not block it. Its cost will mainly be borne by the
City of London, which accounts for three-quarters of the market,
and Luxembourg.

The art market

The theory of raising rivals' costs applies not only to regulation but also to taxation. In the European Union, harmonisation of ordinary taxes requires unanimity in the Council. But the
Commission, at the suggestion of the French government, found a
loophole: the *droit de suite*. The so-called Droit de Suite Directive
of 2001 (officially the 'Directive on the Resale Right for the Benefit
of the Author of an Original Work of Art') obliges art galleries and
auction houses to pay a certain percentage of the resale price to

the artists and their (often distant) heirs. The heirs are entitled to receive a royalty for seventy years after the artist's death. Even though, formally, the *droit de suite* is not a tax, it is effectively equivalent to an earmarked tax.

The *droit de suite* was first introduced in France in 1921. By 2001, it had been copied by ten other EU member states. It does not exist in Switzerland, New York, Hong Kong and most other art centres outside the EU, though UNESCO recommends it. The legislative proposal of the European Commission was immediately opposed by four member states not levying the *droit de suite* (the UK, Ireland, Austria and the Netherlands), which feared for their art markets (Sotheby's, Christie's, etc., in London, the Dorotheum in Vienna, the Maastricht Art Fair, etc.). London at the time hosted 72 per cent of the EU's art market. The four countries were supported by Luxembourg and some Nordic countries, but they failed to assemble a blocking minority. As they could not beat the others, they decided to join them – first of all Austria and the Netherlands, then Ireland and, finally, with some minor concessions, the UK. The duty has been levied since 2006. It will have to be raised and extended to the heirs by 2011 – or 2013 at the latest.

Voting in the Council

Decision-making on these directives ought to be seen in the wider context of the Council's voting record. The available studies have yielded the following results.

In 1994–98, 21 per cent of the legislative acts were openly contested (Mattila and Lane, 2001: Table 1). From December 2001 to October 2006, the share was at least 15 per cent (Hagemann and De Clerk-Sachsse, 2007: 10). As Mattila and Lane show (2001: Table 2), the share of dissenting votes was largest in the field of agriculture (33 per cent), the internal market (30 per cent), transport (27 per cent), public health (23 per cent) and social or labour market policy (17 per cent).

In the nineties, the main contestants were the German, Swedish, British, Italian, Dutch and Danish governments – in that order (ibid.: Table 4). In 2001–04, Portugal and Spain joined this group (Hagemann and DeClerk-Sachsse, 2007: 15). The British government voted 'no' or abstained in 3.7 per cent of all cases in 1994–2000 (Mattila, 2004: Table 1). The countries most likely to join British dissent were Sweden, Denmark, Finland, Ireland and the Netherlands – in that order (Mattila and Lane, 2001: Figure 3). The British negotiating positions were closest to those of Sweden, followed, in order, by Denmark, the Netherlands, Germany, Finland and Austria (Kaeding and Selck, 2005: Figure 5). Since the eastern enlargement, the following new member states have tended to be closest to the British position: Slovakia, Estonia, Latvia, Lithuania, Hungary and the Czech Republic (Hagemann and DeClerk-Sachsse, 2007: Figure 8). In the Council of Ministers on Employment, Social Policy and Consumer Affairs, the governments of Germany, the UK, Luxembourg, the Czech Republic, Poland and Latvia were the most frequent contesters (ibid.: Figure 12).

At least four studies of the pre-2004 Councils identify the North–South division as the main cleavage.[7] A survey of 125 EU experts by Thomson et al. (2004: 255f) reveals the reason for

7   Beyers and Dierickx (1998: 312); Mattila and Lane (2001: 45); Elgstroem et al. (2001: 121); Zimmer et al. (2005). The division has been less pronounced since 2001 (Hagemann and DeClerk-Sachsse, 2007: Figures 3, 6 and 8).

this: 'A clear majority (44 issues or 76 per cent) of the 60 issues where there are significant divisions between Northern and Southern delegations concern choices between free-market and regulatory alternatives ... In general, the Northern delegations tend to support more market-based solutions than the Southern delegations.'

Zimmer et al. (2005: 412), in their analysis of Council voting, reach a similar conclusion: 'As a rule, the results confirm the observation that the poorer Southern member states demand more market regulation, protectionism and redistribution than the Northern member states, who seek increased free trade, market liberalisation and the restriction of EU expenses.'

These findings are highly relevant in predicting the probable consequences of the Lisbon Treaty, if adopted.

How the Lisbon Treaty would affect policy

The Lisbon Treaty alters the country weights and the majority requirement in the Council. The current country weights, which favour the smaller member states relative to the larger ones, are to be replaced by population weights. The majority requirement is to be lowered from 73.9 per cent to 65 per cent in 2017. Moreover, 55 per cent of the member states have to assent – which is even easier to attain. The population threshold is likely to be the binding constraint.

The lowering of the upper majority requirement would render the centralisation of policymaking easier. This is also the hope of the European Commission. I quote from a working paper presented by Commissioner Margot Wallstroem in 2006: 'The Constitution redefines a qualified majority to simplify and facilitate decision-making in the Council ... It would make it easier to reach the qualified majority needed to adopt a proposal. Not only is the qualified majority easier to reach but it is also applied more widely.'[8] Since the European Union is largely, if not mainly, a regulatory body, interference with freedom of contract would increase in all markets. Economically, the Lisbon Treaty would not strengthen the European Union but weaken it from within.

Moreover, the transition to population weights would reduce the voting share of the typical anti-regulation coalition in the Council (the UK, Ireland, the Netherlands and the Scandinavian member states) because, with the exception of the UK, these countries are small countries.

It is hard to see why population weights ought to be used in the Council at all. As the Council represents the states, it is comparable to a second chamber of parliament like the Senate in the USA, the Bundesrat in Germany or the Ständerat in Switzerland. In all these federal chambers, the voting share of the smaller states exceeds their population shares – as in the present EU Council. In this way, the smaller states are protected against domination by the larger states and, ultimately, against political centralisation. Weighting by population, or rather by the size of the electorate, would be appropriate for the European Parliament, but there, as we have seen, it is neither practised nor envisaged.

The main reason that is usually given to justify the lowering of the binding majority requirement is the eastern enlargement, but this argument is dubious for several reasons.

The accession of the eastern states has raised not only the cost of attaining agreement but also the heterogeneity of needs and

---

8   'The cost of the non-constitution', Commission Staff Working Paper, Brussels, 2006, S. 8.

preferences. Never before has the income differential between the old and the incoming members been so large, and never before have the historical traditions been so different. If the differences of preference increase among the member countries, however, the majority requirement ought to be raised, not lowered.

Moreover, the main reason for admitting qualified majority decisions rather than insisting on unanimity is that no single member state ought to be able to maintain its protectionist policies. The government of a member state may try to protect its domestic producers by way of national product or process regulations. Under the unanimity rule, it could do so. To prevent each country from maintaining its protectionist barriers, the majority requirement has to be set at 100 per cent minus the voting weight of the largest member state. Needless to say, this critical level is much higher than the present requirement of 73.9 per cent – perhaps because there may also be protectionist coalitions of two or more governments. But, in any case, the voting share of such a member state or coalition declines as additional countries join and the number of members increases. Thus, the anti-protectionist argument implies that the majority requirement should be *raised* when the European Union is enlarged.

It is also questionable whether the decision rules should be changed again when the eastern enlargement was the main motivation for the Treaty of Nice. Preparing for the enlargement, the EU-15 abandoned the unanimity rule in many policy fields. Did something unexpected happen in the meantime to make further change necessary?

If there has been an unexpected development, it was probably the decline in the share of contested Council decisions since enlargement. The percentage dropped from 17 to 15 per cent

(Hagemann and DeClerk-Sachsse, 2007). At the same time, as Wallace (2007: 5) reports, the number of legislative acts has remained stable at 164 per annum (in 2002/03 and 2005/06). She concludes from her survey of the empirical literature: 'The evidence of practice since May 2004 suggests that the EU's institutional processes and practice have stood up rather robustly to the impact of enlargement' (p. 22) … 'The "business as usual" picture is more convincing than the "gridlock" picture' (p. 4). Thus, the eastern enlargement has not weakened the decision-making capacity of the European Union. The Treaty of Nice is fulfilling its purpose.

Admittedly, our experience of the new regime is still rather limited. The future may be different. But then the decision to change the voting rules ought to be postponed – say, until 2016. The member states should wait and see how the enlargement works out. Their decision would be better informed and more appropriate.

The governments control the size of the budget and the Treaties

The governments of the member states control not only ordinary EU legislation but also the size of the budget and all amendments to the treaties. The budget process is ingenious but the amendment procedure is worth reforming.

The member states decide unanimously about the financing of the European Union. The spending decisions are taken in a different way, however: 'non-compulsory expenditure' is ultimately controlled by the European Parliament, while 'compulsory expenditure' is ultimately determined by the Council, acting by qualified majority. Since a net contributing country cannot prevent the others from spending its money in a way it dislikes, no net contributor is likely to assent to excessive budget increases. This explains why the budget has remained at about 1 per cent of GDP for more than two decades. The asymmetry of the decision rules ensures fiscal restraint. Hence, the European institutions resort to regulation rather than spending: as mentioned at the very beginning, the number of directives has increased twice as much as EU expenditure relative to GNP. Regulation costs the EU institutions very little. Its cost has to be borne by those who have to comply with all these restrictions.

Amendments to the treaties have to be negotiated and proposed by an 'Intergovernmental Conference'. Formally, this is distinguished from the Council but the decision-makers are the same. The governments are the agenda-setters for Treaty amendments, just as the Commission is the agenda-setter for ordinary EU legislation. This is problematic. It means that the national parliaments are not masters of the Treaty. Moreover, since in many respects the governments are more biased towards EU centralisation than the national parliaments, the current amendment procedure generates outcomes that are far from the preferences of citizens.

The political class is aware of these criticisms. In 2002 it called a 'Convention for the Future of Europe', which was to prepare a 'Constitutional Treaty'. This convention was not to replace the Intergovernmental Conference as the agenda-setter, however. It was merely supposed to present a draft to the Intergovernmental Conference.

Only 30 of the 66 convention delegates and merely two of the twelve members of the presidium were national parliamentarians.

The presidium, which had full control over the draft, included two Commissioners, two Euro-parliamentarians, three representatives of the national governments, two national parliamentarians, the president of the Convention (V. Giscard d'Estaing) and two vice-presidents (G. Amato and J. H. Dehaene). The presence of the Commissioners and the Euro-parliamentarians was, of course, incompatible with the fundamental constitutional principle that the rules of the game must not be made by those who will later have to abide by them.

Which members of the presidium held the median position? The president and the two vice-presidents were more Europhile than the national representatives but less interested in centralisation than the EU Commissioners and EU parliamentarians. They occupied the median. Thus, the convention was designed to generate a draft that would be more biased towards centralisation than the Intergovernmental Conference. It was a way of putting public pressure on the less centralisation-prone national governments, especially the British.

The convention was not an exercise in democracy – contrary to the impression the organisers tried to convey. The composition of the assembly and the presidium was corporatist. Moreover, it was arbitrary from the point of view of democratic representation. It was designed to produce a particular outcome.

To render Treaty amendment more democratic, the Intergovernmental Conference ought to be replaced by an Interparliamentary Conference. The Interparliamentary Conference would be called and organised by the second chamber of the EU Parliament which I have proposed above.

The experience of the last few years, however, leaves no doubt that this will not be enough. No national government and no national parliament dared to resist the convention proposal (even though some changes were made). It was only by popular referenda – in France, the Netherlands and Ireland – that the European institutions could be stopped. Should the Treaty itself prescribe such referenda?

There is a dilemma. On the one hand, unbiased decisions will be delivered only by the sovereign himself – the people. On the other hand, the citizens may be less well informed than the politicians, and the treaties should not unnecessarily interfere with the constitutional practices of the member states. There is a case for a compromise: the treaties might oblige the member states to call referenda on all amendments, but the national constitutions would determine whether the popular vote is binding.

5 THE EUROPEAN COURT OF JUSTICE

The European Court of Justice (ECJ) is often called a 'motor' of European integration. It has been a driving force of both market and political integration. In particular, it has invented various doctrines, such as the primacy and the direct-effects doctrines, which are not contained in the treaties. Nor are they inevitable. The primacy of EU law, for example, has been expressly excluded in the Take-over Directive of 2003. Its provisions apply only in member states that do not legislate otherwise. The Court has also conferred powers on the European Parliament which are not provided for in the treaties.

The Court is increasingly criticised for its centralising bias.[1] A court should not propagate a political programme – it ought to be an objective and impartial interpreter of the law.

The European Court is the supreme court of the European Union – a quasi-constitutional court. It shares its centralising bias with most national constitutional courts, most notably in federal states.[2] In the early years of the United States of America,

---

1   See, for example, Schermers (1974); Stein (1981); Philip (1983); Rasmussen (1986); Bzdera (1992); Burley and Mattli (1993); Weiler (1999); Garrett (1993); Neill (1995); Bednar et al. (1996); Garrett et al. (1998); Pitarakis and Tridimas (2003); Voigt (2003); and Josselin and Marciano (2007).

2   Von Brünneck (1988); Bzdera (1992); Vaubel (1996); and Chalmers (2004). Von Brünneck, a German professor of constitutional law, concludes from an international comparison of constitutional reviews in Western democracies:

the Supreme Court under Chief Justice John Marshall behaved in a very similar way. An international cross-sectional analysis (Vaubel, 1996) showed that the age of the constitutional court is a major determinant of the centralisation of government expenditure in federal states.

Why do constitutional courts tend to centralise? Four explanations ought to be considered.

Explaining the centralist bias

First, the constitutional judges may depend on the politicians who have chosen them. I call this the dependency hypothesis. The judges may be dependent because they want to be reappointed. The ECJ judges have a term of six years but on average they stay 9.3 years (Voigt, 2003). Thus, the probability of being reappointed exceeds 50 per cent. According to this hypothesis, the judges centralise because the governments want them to do so. The politicians let the Court do the centralisation because they do not want to be considered responsible by the voters. Moreover, the judges can change the meaning of the treaties by simple majority vote whereas amendments to the treaties would require a unanimous vote of all member states, and ratification by the national parliaments or even referenda. A cross-sectional analysis of national constitutional courts (Vaubel, 2009), however, reveals that federal government shares of total government expenditure are higher when constitutional judges enjoy a greater degree of

'Constitutional courts predominantly tend to expand the power of central institutions in the economic sector' (p. 236). His conclusion is supported by case studies for the USA, Germany, Austria, Australia, post-1948 Canada and India (for a survey see Vaubel, 1996). Chalmers writes: 'Central judicial institutions almost invariably have centralising rather than particularist tendencies' (p. 63).

independence. It would seem that political independence, not dependence, causes centralisation.

Second, the judges may centralise not because they depend on the politicians but because they share the politicians' preferences. The politicians choose judges who share their preference for centralisation. Once more, centralisation may be easier for the judges than for the politicians. The 'shared-preference hypothesis' is consistent with the fact that the share of central government expenditure is lower in those federal states in which one half of the constitutional judges are chosen by representatives of the lower-level governments. But it does not explain why judicial independence leads to centralisation.

Third, the Court, like the European Parliament, may suffer from self-selection bias. While the first two hypotheses are demand-side explanations focusing on the wishes of the politicians, this is a supply-side explanation: the experts eligible for appointment to the ECJ are lawyers who believe in centralisation rather than subsidiarity. That is why they have been specialising in EU law. The self-selection hypothesis explains why judicial independence leads to centralisation. At the level of the national constitutional courts, it also explains why the share of central government is larger if the barriers to constitutional amendment are high.[3] The politicians entitled to amend the constitution find it difficult to override, i.e. correct, unwelcome decisions of the constitutional court.

Fourth, the ECJ judges, like the Commissioners and members of the European Parliament, may have a vested interest in centralisation at the European level because it increases their influence

---

3   The effect is statistically significant (Vaubel, 2009).

and prestige. The larger the powers of the European institutions and the larger therefore the extent of EU legislation and administration, the more important and interesting are the cases that the ECJ judges will be entitled to decide. For example, constitutional courts have to adjudicate inter-institutional disputes at the same level of government. As long as the policy competence belongs to the member states, these disputes are not decided by the ECJ but by the national constitutional courts. But once the competence is transferred to the European level, the judges of the ECJ will be in charge.

Like the self-selection hypothesis, the vested-interest explanation is consistent with the fact that centralisation bears a significant positive correlation with both judicial independence and the difficulty of amending the constitution.

Reforming the Court

It is not easy to correct ECJ decisions by legislative override. In theory, they may be overturned by ordinary legislation or by amending the treaties. Ordinary legislation, however, requires, first, a proposal from the Commission, which shares the Court's vested interest in centralisation; second, depending on the issue, a qualified majority or unanimity in the Council; and, third, also depending on the issue, the assent of the European Parliament, which shares the Court's vested interest as well. In practice it is therefore impossible to override ECJ decisions by ordinary legislation.

Reversal by Treaty amendment requires agreement among all member governments at an Intergovernmental Conference and ratification by all member parliaments. This means that the judges are free to decide as they wish as long as they enjoy the support of at least one national government or one national parliament. As a result, the Court's decisions are hardly ever reversed by Treaty amendments.[4]

What can be done to facilitate legislative override? If the Court has reinterpreted secondary law, the Council may be given the right to reverse the decision without a proposal from the Commission and without the assent of the European Parliament, since both share the Court's vested interest in centralisation. If the Court has reinterpreted the Treaty, the parliaments of the member states or the second chamber of the European Parliament may be given the right to reverse the decision without an Intergovernmental Conference or even by majority. Curbing the Court's influence, however, is merely trying to control the damage – it does not remove the roots of the problem.

Since the ECJ judges are appointed by the governments of the member states, the centralist bias of the ECJ is not due to dependency on EU institutions. The Court could be made even more dependent on the national governments by requiring publication of the voting record. But the optimal solution is not to introduce new and better biases but to get rid of all biases. Courts ought to be neutral interpreters of the law.

Instead of introducing other biases or merely controlling the damage, the reform ought to go to the roots of the problem: the self-selection bias and the Court's vested interest in centralisation.

Self-selection may be limited by requiring judicial experience.

4   A rare exception is the so-called Barber Protocol of the Maastricht Treaty, which overturned the Court's decision in the so-called Barber case of 1989 (262/88, ECR I-1989). The Court had ruled that sex-based differences in pensionable ages had to be eliminated.

In the past, a minority of the lawyers appointed to the ECJ had previously served in a judicial function in their home country (Kuhn, 1993: 195). At present, 14 of the 27 judges meet this condition. Most of the others have been professors or civil servants. The President of the Court, Vassilios Skouris, has been a professor and Minister of the Interior in two socialist Greek governments. He lacks judicial experience.

According to the treaties (Article 223 TEC), the judges shall 'possess the qualifications required for the appointment to the highest judicial offices in their respective countries or [be] jurisconsults of recognised competence'. As Nugent (1999: 272f) has put it, however, 'governments have tended not to be overly worried about the judicial qualifications or experience of their nominations'.

To narrow the choice further, the judges should have to be drawn from the highest courts of the member states, provided that they have gained judicial experience before being appointed to the national constitutional court. This would minimise self-selection, maximise the judicial competence of the European judges and improve the integration of EU and national constitutional law.[5]

The Court's vested interest in centralisation is due to the fact that it is responsible for two tasks at the same time: (i) the task of allocating powers between the member states and the European Union; and (ii) the task of interpreting EU law within those powers. The solution, therefore, is to separate these tasks and to

5   The legal interpretations of the ECJ and the highest national courts should also be linked more closely by abolishing the preliminary reference procedure. The latter enables the lower courts of the member states to appeal directly to the ECJ, bypassing the highest national courts.

have two European courts: one court that has no power other than adjudicating cases concerning the division of labour between the member states and the EU – call it the Subsidiarity Court – and one court that decides all other cases.

To avoid self-selection, the judges of the Subsidiarity Court ought to have served on their national constitutional court. Indeed, each might be delegated by his or her national court and return to it when the term at the Subsidiarity Court is over.[6]

If this proposal were put into practice, it would not be necessary to publish the voting record of the judges or facilitate legislative override. The most effective solution is not to deprive the judges of their independence and influence but to correct their incentives. That is the economic approach.

Neither the Constitutional Treaty (2004) nor the Lisbon Treaty (2007) contains any of these reforms. Instead, they provide for a panel of seven persons, among them at least one member of a national supreme court, who shall give an opinion on candidates' qualification for the ECJ (Article III-357 CT and Article 255 of the Treaty on the Future of the European Union – TFEU – respectively). This will not make much of a difference. But it indicates that the governments of the member states have sensed the pressure for reforming the European Court of Justice.

6   Some sort of Subsidiarity Court has been proposed by several authors, including the European Constitutional Group (since 1993) and Weiler (1999: 353f).

6 LISBON AND THE ALTERNATIVES

The Treaty of Lisbon has strengths and weaknesses. The weaknesses are serious, however, while the strengths are minor. On balance, the Treaty makes existing problems worse. It reinforces the centralising dynamic.

Positive aspects of the Treaty

I start with the improvements – those that might be worth mentioning.

First, Article 50 of the Amended Treaty on the European Union (ATEU) explicitly mentions the right to withdraw from the EU. This right has always existed but some authors have denied it. All treaties, indeed all contracts, may be terminated in some way. As the example of Canada demonstrates, there may even be constitutional arrangements for secession. The American Civil War has shown, however, that it is important to explicate as clearly as possible whether and how a member state may withdraw from the European Union. Article 50 ATEU prescribes negotiations with the aim of concluding an agreement but, failing that, the treaties would cease to apply to the withdrawing state two years after it has notified the EU of its intention to withdraw. In comparison with current law, the Treaty of Lisbon delays the withdrawal but the markets need a pre-announcement anyhow so that they have time to adjust. Thus, in sum, this article is an improvement.

Second, Article 6, Section 2 ATEU obliges the EU to join the European Convention for the Protection of Human Rights and Fundamental Freedoms, which was negotiated in 1950 and entered into force in 1953. By now, the convention has been signed by 47 European states and is enforced by a court in Strasbourg. It should not be confused with the EU Charter of Fundamental Rights of 2000, which will be enforced by the European Court of Justice (ECJ) in Luxembourg and which is formally recognised by the Lisbon Treaty (Article 6, Section 1 ATEU). Unlike the EU Charter, the European Convention focuses on negative rights, i.e. freedom, rather than positive rights, i.e. claims to government regulations and transfers. It is not a coincidence that the word 'freedom' is mentioned in the title of the European Convention but not that of the EU Charter. Moreover, with regard to negative rights, a court controlled by 47 member states is likely to provide more effective protection to a minority within the EU than a court controlled by the EU majority. In the Strasbourg court, the EU majority may easily be a minority. Accession to the Strasbourg convention is, however, not of first-order importance – given that the individual member states have already signed up.

Third, Article 15, Section 5 ATEU extends the term of the president of the Council from six months to two and a half years. This amendment, proposed by the former French president Jacques Chirac, would strengthen the Council vis-à-vis the other EU institutions, especially the Commission. Moreover, the Council presidency would no longer rotate among all member states – so the larger member states would be more likely to gain the presidency. This would increase the weight of the Council as well. But the Council would not receive any additional powers vis-à-vis the other EU institutions.

Fourth, there is a Protocol on the Application of the Principles of Subsidiarity and Proportionality which makes the national parliaments guardians of the subsidiarity principle. It is a thoroughly diluted version of a proposal by Valéry Giscard d'Estaing, the president of the Convention for the Future of Europe. According to Article 6 of the protocol, 'any national parliament or any chamber of a national Parliament may, within eight weeks from the date of transmission of a draft legislative act, in the official languages of the Union, send to the Presidents of the European Parliament, the Council and the Commission a reasoned opinion stating why it considers that the draft in question does not comply with the principle of subsidiarity'.

Article 7 continues:

> Where reasoned opinions on a draft legislative act's non-compliance with the principle of subsidiarity represent at least one third of all the votes allocated to the national Parliaments ... the draft must be reviewed ... Each national Parliament will have two votes ... In the case of a bicameral Parliamentary system, each of the two chambers shall have one vote ... After such review, the Commission or, where appropriate, the group of Member States, the European Parliament, the Court of Justice, the European Central Bank or the European Investment Bank, if the draft legislative act originates from them, may decide to maintain, amend or withdraw the draft. Reasons must be given for this decision.

Four features of this provision are worth noting: (i) It is not in the main text of the Treaty but in a protocol. Apparently, the drafters did not think that it is important – which is true. (ii) The national parliaments have eight weeks to voice their concern. That is a tight constraint. It means that the drafters want to make it difficult for the national parliaments to complain. (iii) There is a majority requirement. This is unusual for legal complaints. If a party to a contract believes that one of the other parties has violated its contractual obligations, each party has the right to complain on its own. (iv) The institution that has proposed the draft legislative act – initially the Commission – may maintain its proposal as long as it gives reasons.

According to Section 3 of Article 7, special provisions apply if the complaints 'represent at least a simple majority of the votes allocated to the national Parliaments'. In this case, the European Parliament and the Council (also called 'the legislator') would have to be involved: 'If, by a majority of 55% of the members of the Council or a majority of the votes cast in the European Parliament, the legislator is of the opinion that the proposal is not compatible with the principle of subsidiarity, the legislative proposal shall not be given further consideration.' This condition makes no difference at all because, under the co-decision procedure of the Lisbon Treaty, the adoption of a legislative act requires a majority of 55 per cent of the Council members and a simple majority in the European Parliament anyhow. If the condition just quoted from the Protocol is satisfied, the draft legislative act has no chance of being adopted anyway. The condition does not add anything that is not already contained in the standard legislative procedure.

Indeed, the national parliaments have always been free to voice their discontent with breaches of the subsidiarity principle. What is new and good is merely that they will get an answer from the Commission if there are many of them.

Finally, Article 8 of the Protocol mentions the fact that 'the Court of Justice of the European Union shall have jurisdiction in actions on grounds of infringement of the principle of subsidiarity by a legislative act' and that it may be notified by the member states 'in accordance with their legal order on behalf of their national Parliament or a chamber thereof'. This has always been the case. Unfortunately, it does not work because the legal orders of the member states do not give their parliaments the right to go to the European Court and because the ECJ shares the interest of the Commission and therefore almost always sides with it against the member states.[1]

Whoever claims that this protocol gives more power, i.e. some sort of control, to the national parliaments is misleading the public. It has no teeth.

What are the alternatives? A majority of the national parliaments may be given the right to veto EU legislation on grounds of the subsidiarity principle. Or the second chamber of the European Parliament proposed in Chapter 3 may obtain this right as suggested. Which is better? It is easier to mobilise the majority of the deputies of a second chamber into action than fourteen national parliaments – especially if there are very restrictive deadlines. If the deputies are chosen by lot so as to exclude self-selection, the second chamber is more effective than relying on the national parliaments.

Fifth, Article 5, Section 3 ATEU improves the definition of subsidiarity. It no longer pretends that all objectives that cannot

---

[1]   The evidence collected by Jupille (2004: Figure 17) demonstrates that 'the ECJ finds in favour of the Commission far more frequently than it rules against it, the opposite applies for the Council, and the EP presents a mixed profile in this respect' (p. 98).

be sufficiently achieved by the member states can be better achieved at the Union level. The comparison should not only be between individual member-state action and European Union action, however: it should also include policies carried out in smaller groupings and methods of coordination that do not require the passage of EU laws.

Sixth, as has been mentioned in Chapter 5, Article 225 ATEC provides for a panel of seven persons, among them at least one member of a national supreme court, who shall give an opinion on candidates' suitability for the European Court of Justice. The European judges would, however, still be chosen by the governments of the member states. What is required is a Subsidiarity Court (see Chapter 5).

These six improvements are worth noting but they do not make much difference. By contrast, some of the changes for the worse are extremely worrying.

Negative aspects of the Treaty

First, the general empowering clause of Article 308 TEC is to be extended from common market matters to all EU policies. The new so-called 'flexibility clause' or 'passerelle clause' (Article 352 TFEU) reads as follows:

> 1. If action by the Union should prove necessary, within the framework of the policies defined in the Treaties, to attain one of the objectives set out in the Treaties, *and the Treaties have not provided the necessary powers*, the Council, acting unanimously on a proposal from the Commission and after obtaining the consent of the European Parliament, shall adopt the appropriate measures ...

> 2. ... The Commission shall draw national Parliaments'
> attention to proposals based on this article ... [emphasis added]

For comparison, the corresponding current Article 308 TEC starts this way: 'If action by the Community should prove necessary to attain, in the course of the operation of the common market, one of the objectives of the Community and the Treaties have not provided the necessary powers ... '

Whereas under the current treaty, the so-called 'Kompetenz Kompetenz' is limited to actions in the course of the operation of the common market, it would under the Lisbon Treaty apply to all actions within the framework of EU policies. Thus, the proposed amendment would deprive the national parliaments of any control over the exercise of any EU power granted within the framework of EU policies. All restrictions of EU powers within the various EU policy fields could be removed against the will of the national parliaments. They would lose all control over the general competencies that they share with the EU.

In the past, the general empowering clause has been used very frequently – more than thirty times per annum. In the words of the Council's legal services, the clause 'has been widely interpreted by the Institutions in order to cover all purposes and objects coming within the general framework of the Treaty and not only those listed in Article 3 TEC' (i.e. the list enumerating the 21 EC activities).[2] Joseph Weiler, a professor of law at Harvard University, has criticised the EU for its 'profligate legislative practices' in the usage of the general empowering clause (1999: 319). The clause was designed to permit more market integration, removing

---

2   Opinion of the Legal Service, European Council, Brussels, 22 June 2007.

national barriers and enhancing individual freedom and market competition. The amended version would open the floodgates for political integration, i.e. centralisation, thus threatening individual freedom and political competition, and it would be subject to even more abuse.

The amended clause contains two further changes: the European Parliament has to assent, and the national parliaments have to be informed. This will not make any difference, however. As has been shown, the European Parliament would assent because it has a vested interest in doing so, and the national parliaments have no use for such information because they lack the power to stop abuses of the general empowering clause.

This amendment must not enter into force. Even more importantly, the abuses of the current version of the clause have to be prevented. The Subsidiarity Court and the second chamber of the European Parliament would have the incentive and power to do this.

Second, the Lisbon Treaty explicitly extends the competencies of the European Union to and in a number of fields, for example coordination of employment, social and health policies (Articles 156, para. 2 and 168, no. 2), sport (Article 165, Section 2), research and technological change (Article 181, Section 2), space policy (Article 189), energy (Article 194), tourism (Article 195), civil protection (Article 196) and administrative cooperation (Article 197). None of these should be a core function of a European Union. The extensions are not dramatic but the tendency of giving ever more powers to the European Union is worrying – especially in conjunction with the new empowering clause. In energy policy, for example, there seem to be some aspects – such as international negotiations with oil- and gas-exporting countries and the pipeline network – which are usefully coordinated among the EU-27. But this does not mean that all aspects of energy policy should fall within the reach of EU institutions. Since energy policy is a shared power, EU action takes precedence over national action, and if EU action in this field is somehow limited by the Treaty, these limits may be removed with reference to the general empowering clause even though the national parliaments have not granted the powers that would be required.

The transfer of additional powers to the European Union is not supported by a majority of citizens. A poll in 2007 showed that only 28 per cent of the respondents want to give more powers to the EU, while 41 per cent are in favour of taking away powers from the EU.[3] Moreover, 75 per cent said that any treaty giving more powers to the EU should require a referendum. This was the majority opinion in each of the 27 member states.

Third, Article 6 ATEU gives the Charter of Fundamental Rights of the European Union 'the same legal value as the Treaty'. The Charter had been adopted in 2000 as a non-binding declaration. The Charter contains not only negative rights, protecting the individual against state power, but also positive rights, establishing claims on the government, such as housing assistance or a free placement service, and a host of regulations – most notably a right to 'fair and just working conditions' (Article 31, no. 1). These claims will be interpreted by the European Court of Justice. Since they are binding, they are likely to become a driving force of labour market regulation. The UK has opted out – but for how long?

A Charter of Fundamental Rights, indeed the treaties themselves, ought to affirm individual freedom of contract. Instead of

---

3   Open Europe, Poll on the Future of Europe, 2007.

requiring regulations, the Charter should protect citizens against government regulations restricting this freedom.

Fourth, the Lisbon Treaty (Article 16, Section 3 ATEU) lowers the binding majority requirement for qualified majority decisions of the Council from 73.9 to 65 per cent. The consequences have been analysed in Chapter 4. The amendment would significantly raise the probability of EU regulation. The majority requirement for EU regulation ought to be raised, not lowered.

Fifth, the Lisbon Treaty abandons the unanimity principle in dozens of fields. The Treaty of Amsterdam and the Treaty of Nice had done the same but to a smaller extent. Moreover, the marginal cost of doing so is rising. Unanimity protects minorities against the tyranny of the majority. It is the sole safeguard against the strategy of raising rivals' costs by common regulations or (quasi-)taxation such as the *droit de suite*.

Sixth, the Lisbon Treaty gives the European Court jurisdiction over the European Central Bank, police and judicial cooperation in criminal matters and parts of the common foreign and security policy. It enables the Court to interpret these sections of the Treaty in a centralising fashion.

There are many more problems with the Lisbon Treaty – for example, regarding the primacy of EU law, the objective of free and undistorted competition and the statute of the European Central Bank – but these examples must suffice. The indubitable bottom line is that the Treaty would reinforce and aggravate the process of European centralisation.

7 THE OUTLOOK

Fourteen years ago, in my IEA monograph *The Centralisation of Western Europe*, I ventured to predict that the pace of political centralisation at the European level would slow down in the future. I still think this will happen but it is taking longer than I expected. Was Maastricht the turning point as I thought it might be? Certainly not. The Treaty of Amsterdam continued on the pathway to the European superstate and the UK joined the Social Agreement. Then, in 1998, eleven member states decided to adopt the euro. The Treaty of Nice strengthened the European Parliament and further reduced the role of the unanimity principle. But Jacques Chirac managed to raise the majority requirement in the Council (from 71.3 to 73.9 per cent) in the event of eastern enlargement. Moreover, the Treaty of Nice was initially rejected by the Irish in a referendum. Also by popular vote, the Danes and the Swedes rejected the euro in 2000 and 2003, respectively. In Germany, the loss of the Deutschmark was deeply resented and clearly led to the government's landslide defeat in the general election of September 1998. Everywhere, popular opposition to ever closer unification has been growing.

The clearest evidence so far, however, has been the widespread resistance to the ill-fated Constitutional Treaty and its travesty, the Treaty of Lisbon. The referenda in France, the Netherlands and Ireland, and the opinion polls elsewhere, leave no doubt that, in many member states, citizens no longer accept the lead that the politicians would like to provide. This is a new situation. Even if the Lisbon Treaty were finally ratified, the process leading there will have been so painful for the Euro-establishment that I do not foresee any further attempts to centralise by Treaty amendment for many years to come.

In 1995, I expressed the hope that the need to accommodate the eastern European countries might act as a brake on centralisation. The eastern enlargement is likely to continue – though at a slower pace – regardless of whether the Lisbon Treaty is ratified or not. But there is no evidence that the eastern Europeans dislike EU centralisation. As we noted above, they are more satisfied with democracy at the EU level than in their home countries. More specifically, they have much more confidence in the European Parliament than in their national parliaments, and also much more confidence in the Council and the Commission than in their national governments[1] – which is not true for the old member states (EU-15). Similarly, the eastern European member states contest Council decisions only half as often as the other countries.[2]

Several explanations come to mind. Certainly, most eastern Europeans are dissatisfied with the slow progress of their home countries. To some extent, political life is still marred by corruption and the legacy of the communist past. And being new, they do not know very much about the realities of the European Union. Their politicians are still learning how to behave in EU

---

[1] According to the Eurobarometer of spring 2006, about 42 per cent of the respondents in the twelve new member states had more confidence in the European Parliament against about 6 per cent who placed more trust in their national parliament. For the Council and Commission versus the national government, the figures were 39 per cent and 9 per cent, respectively.

[2] Dehousse and Gaudez (2006).

institutions. Furthermore, they are net recipients from the EU budget. They are grateful for, but also dependent on, EU support. They do not dare to object. This situation will persist for some time.

For these reasons, the initiative for reform is more likely to come from some of the old member states – especially net contributing countries such as the UK, the Netherlands, Sweden, France, Austria, Denmark and Finland.[3]

In my 1995 paper, I argued that the initiative for reforming the European institutions would have to come from the parliaments of the member states. I no longer believe that they are up to the challenge. Under normal conditions, the backbenchers are captives of the cabinet. Only the imminent prospect of electoral defeat may induce the majority of parliamentarians to revolt against the government and force it to do what they want. Only the electorate may impose a fundamental reform through referenda and party competition. But voters are slow to learn about the EU. It will take some time before European issues play an important or even a dominant role in national elections. Is there anything that can be done in the meantime?

The governments of the member states, assembled in the Council, share a common interest: to increase the power of the Council relative to the other EU institutions. They also hold the key to amending the treaties. The national parliaments willingly ratify amendments proposed by the governments, and the assent of the European Parliament is not (yet?) required. The fact that

---

3   Except for the UK, I have listed these countries in the order of their net contributions relative to GDP (2005). Luxembourg, Germany, Italy and Belgium, in this order, are also net contributors, but for various reasons they seem less likely to take the initiative.

the Constitutional Treaty and the Lisbon Treaty both strengthen the Council by extending the term of the Council presidency proves that the Council is interested in increasing its influence (and able to do so).

The European institutions compete for power. The following reforms are in the interest of all Council members:

- Shift competencies from the Commission to the Council. The most obvious starting point is the removal of the Commission's monopoly on legislative initiative. Extend the right of initiative to the Council and the European Parliament. On this issue, the Council would even have the support of the European Parliament. Next, strip the Commission of its non-executive functions. Establish an independent competition authority. Finally, subordinate the Commission's executive functions to the Council so that the Commission gradually becomes a normal civil service. If the Belgian government defends the interests of the Commission, offer concessions to Belgium in some other field.

- Limit the power and centralist bias of the European Court of Justice. The Council members will not be interested in setting up a Subsidiarity Court whose judges are delegated from the highest national courts rather than chosen by the governments themselves. But the Council members do not want the ECJ to be an independent and uncontrollable motor of centralisation. They are likely to see the merit of separating the subsidiarity cases from the normal business of a European Court. They will like the idea of a Subsidiarity Court whose judges are nominated by the governments of the member states. In any case, they are interested to know how the individual judges have voted in each case. If the government of Luxembourg defends the interests of the ECJ judges, offer concessions to Luxembourg in some other field.

• Remove the blocking power of the European Parliament with regard to decentralising legislation. The members of the Council stand to benefit from having a second chamber of the European Parliament which would be entitled to repatriate powers if and where necessary. Moreover, if the parliamentarians of the second chamber are at the same time members of the national parliaments, they are more accessible to the wishes of the governments, assembled in the Council, than the members of the first chamber.

A major part of the required reforms may be initiated by the Council, even though this is not the short-run outlook. But from a public choice perspective, a positive reform of the European institutions is clearly possible within the foreseeable future. Many nation-states have found ways to decentralise government spending in the last few decades.[4] There is no iron law of centralisation.

---

4 Vaubel (2008: Table A.1) shows the evolution of the share of central government expenditure in total government expenditure in 43 countries from the first half of the 1970s to the period 2001–04. Among the EU-15 (excluding Luxembourg), the share of central government has declined in nine countries (percentage-point changes in parentheses): Spain (–11.9), Italy (–9.8), Denmark (–8.7), Belgium (–7.9), Portugal (–6.6), the Netherlands (–4.5), Sweden (–2.5), Finland (–2.0) and France (–1.3). The main centralisers have been the UK (+8.5), Germany (+6.3) and Austria (+6.0).

REFERENCES

Alesina, A., I. Agnelloni and L. Schuknecht (2005), 'What does the European Union do?', *Public Choice*, 123: 275–319.

Andersen, S. S. and K. A. Eliassen (1991), 'European Community lobbying', *European Journal of Political Research*, 20: 173–87.

Attali, J. (1995), *Verbatim III*, Paris: Fayard.

Bednar, J., J. Ferejohn and G. Garrett (1996), 'Politics of European federalism', *International Review of Law and Economics*, 16: 279–94.

Bernholz, P. and R. Vaubel (eds) (2007), *Political Competition and Economic Regulation*, London: Routledge.

Beyers, J. C. M. and G. Dierickx (1998), 'The working groups of the Council of the European Union: supranational or intergovernmental negotiations?', *Journal of Common Market Studies*, 36: 289–317.

Boockmann, B. and R. Vaubel (2009), 'The theory of raising rivals' costs and evidence from the International Labour Organisation', *World Economy* (forthcoming).

Botero, J., S. Djankov, R. de la Porta, F. Lopez-de-Silanes and A. Schliefer (2004), 'The regulation of labor', *Quarterly Journal of Economics*, 118: 1339–82.

Burley, A.-M. and W. Mattli (1993), 'Europe before the court: a political theory of legal integration', *International Organization*, 47: 41–76.

Bzdera, A. (1992), 'The Court of Justice of the European Community and the politics of institutional reform', *West European Politics*, 15: 122–36.

Chalmers, D. (2004), 'The legal dimension of European integration', in A. M. El-Agraa (ed.), *The European Union*, Harlow: Pearson and Prentice-Hall, pp. 57–75.

Dehousse, R. and D. Gaudez (2006), 'Vers une banalisation du vote au Conseil?', in R. Dehousse and D. Gaudez (eds), *Élargissement: comment l'Europe s'adapte*, Paris: Science Po, Les Presses.

Dreher, A. and R. Vaubel (2004), 'Do IMF and IBRD cause moral hazard and political business cycles? Evidence from panel data', *Open Economies Review*, 15: 5–22.

Dyson, K. and K. Featherstone (1999), *The Road to Maastricht*, Oxford: Oxford University Press.

Elgstroem, O., B. Bjurulf, J. Johansson and A. Sannersted (2001), 'Coalitions in European Union negotiations', *Scandinavian Political Studies*, 24: 111–28.

European Constitutional Group (2007), *A Revised European Constitutional Treaty*, European Constitutional Group website.

Falke, J. (1996), 'Comitology and other committees. A preliminary empirical assessment', in R. H. Pedler and G. F. Schäfer (eds), *Shaping European Law and Policy: The Role of Committees and Comitology in the Political Process*, Maastricht: European Institute of Public Administration, pp. 132ff.

Favier, P. and M. Martin-Roland (1996), *La Décennie Mitterrand*, vol. 3: *Les Défis*, Paris: Seuil.

Fisman, R. and R. Gatti (2002), 'Decentralization and corruption: evidence across countries', *Journal of Public Economics*, 83: 325–45.

Garrett, G. (1993), 'The politics of legal integration in the European Union', *International Organization*, 49: 171–81.

Garrett, G., D. Kelemen and H. Schulz (1998), 'The European Court of Justice, national governments and legal integration in the European Union', *International Organization*, 52: 149–76.

Gillingham, J. (2003), *European Integration 1950–2003: Superstate or New Market Economy?*, Cambridge: Cambridge University Press.

Gwartney, J. and R. Lawson (2004), *Economic Freedom in the World*, Annual Report, Vancouver: Fraser Institute.

Hagemann, S. and J. De Clerk-Sachsse (2007), *Old Rules, New Game: Decision-Making in the Council of Ministers after the 2004 Enlargement*, Special Report, Brussels: Centre for Economic Policy Studies, March.

Haller, M. (2008), *European Integration as an Elite Process*, London: Routledge.

Josselin, J.-M. and A. Marciano (2007), 'How the Court made a federation of the EU', *Review of International Organizations*, 2: 59–76.

Jupille, J. (2004), *Procedural Politics: Issues, Interests and Institutional Choice in the European Union*, Cambridge: Cambridge University Press.

Kaeding, M. and T. J. Selck (2005), 'Mapping out political Europe: coalition patterns in EU decision making', *International Political Science Review*, 26: 271–90.

König, T., B. Luetgert and T. Dannwolf (2006), 'Quantifying European legislative research', *European Union Politics*, 7: 553–74.

Kuhn, B. (1993), *Sozialraum Europa: Zentralisierung oder Dezentralisierung der Sozialpolitik?*, Idstein.

Mattila, M. (2004), 'Contested decisions: empirical analysis of voting in the European Union Council of Ministers', *European Journal of Political Research*, 43: 29–50.

Mattila, M. and J.-E. Lane (2001), 'Why unanimity in the Council? A roll call analysis of Council voting', *European Union Politics*, 2: 31–52.

Neill, P. (1995), *The European Court of Justice: A Case Study in Judicial Activism*, London: European Policy Forum.

Nickell, S. and L. Nunziata (2001), *Labour Institutions Data Base*, London: London School of Economics website.

Noury, A. G. and G. Roland (2002), 'More power to the European Parliament?', *Economic Policy*, 17: 281–319.

Nugent, N. (1999), *The Government and Politics of the European Union*, 4th edn, Basingstoke: Macmillan.

O'Reilly, J., B. Reissert and V. Eichener (1996), 'European regulation of social standards: social security, working time, workplace participation, occupational health and safety', in G. Schmid, J. O'Reilly and K. Schönemann (eds), *International Handbook of Labour Market Policy Evaluation*, Cheltenham: Edward Elgar, pp. 868–98.

Organisation for Economic Cooperation and Development, *OECD Employment Outlook*, Paris.

Peirce, W. (1991), 'Unanimous decisions in a redistributive context: the Council of Ministers of the European Communities', in R. Vaubel and T. D. Willett (eds), *The*

Political Economy of International Organizations: A Public Choice Approach, Boulder, CO: Westview Press, pp. 267–85.

Philip, C. (1983), *La Cour de Justice des Communautés Européennes*, Paris: Presses Universitaires de France.

Pitarakis, J.-Y. and G. Tridimas (2003), 'Joint dynamics of legal economic integration in the European Union', *European Journal of Law and Economics*, 16: 357–68.

Quatremer, J. and T. Klau (1999), *Ces hommes qui ont fait l'euro*, Paris: Plon.

Rasmussen, H. (1986), *On Law and Policy in the European Court of Justice*, Dordrecht: Nijhoff.

Schermers, H. (1974), 'The European Court of Justice: promoter of European integration', *American Journal of Comparative Law*, 22: 444–64.

Schmitt, H. and J. Thomassen (eds) (1999), *Political Representation and Legitimacy in the European Union*, Oxford: Oxford University Press.

Stein, E. (1981), 'Lawyers, judges and the making of a transnational constitution', *American Journal of International Law*, 75: 1–27.

Teltschik, H. (1991), *Innenansichten der Einigung*, Berlin: Siedler.

Thomson, R., J. Bourefijn and F. Stokman (2004), 'Actor alignments in European decision-making', *European Journal of Political Research*, 43: 237–61.

Vaubel, R. (1996), 'Constitutional safeguards against centralization in federal states: an international cross-section analysis', *Constitutional Political Economy*, 7: 79–102.

Vaubel, R. (2002), 'Geschichtsforschungen zu dem Buch *The Road to Maastricht* (K. Dyson, K. Featherstone)', *Kredit und Kapital*, 35: 460–70.

Vaubel, R. (2004), 'Federation with majority decisions: economic lessons from the history of the United States, Germany and the European Union', *Economic Affairs*, 24: 53–9.

Vaubel, R. (2008), 'The political economy of labour market regulation by the European Union', *Review of International Organizations*, 3: 435–65.

Vaubel, R. (2009), 'Constitutional Courts as Promoters of Political Centralization: Lessons for the European Court of Justice', Manuscript, University of Mannheim.

Voigt, S. (2003), 'Iudex calculat: the ECJ's quest for power', *Jahrbuch für Neue Politische Ökonomie*, 22: 77–101.

Von Brünneck, A. (1988), 'Constitutional review and legislation in Western democracies', in C. Landfried (ed.), *Constitutional Review and Legislation: An International Comparison*, Baden-Baden: Nomos.

Wallace, H. (2007), *Adapting to Enlargement in the European Union: Institutional Practice since May 2004*, Report, Brussels: Trans-European Policy Studies Association (TEPSA), 16 November.

Weiler, J. H. H. (1999), *The Constitution of Europe*, Cambridge: Cambridge University Press.

Zimmer, C., G. Schneider and M. Dobbins (2005), 'The contested Council: the conflict dimensions of an intergovernmental institution', *Political Studies*, 53: 403–22.

ABOUT THE IEA

The Institute is a research and educational charity (No. CC 235 351), limited by guarantee. Its mission is to improve understanding of the fundamental institutions of a free society by analysing and expounding the role of markets in solving economic and social problems.

The IEA achieves its mission by:

- a high-quality publishing programme
- conferences, seminars, lectures and other events
- outreach to school and college students
- brokering media introductions and appearances

The IEA, which was established in 1955 by the late Sir Antony Fisher, is an educational charity, not a political organisation. It is independent of any political party or group and does not carry on activities intended to affect support for any political party or candidate in any election or referendum, or at any other time. It is financed by sales of publications, conference fees and voluntary donations.

In addition to its main series of publications the IEA also publishes a quarterly journal, *Economic Affairs*.

The IEA is aided in its work by a distinguished international Academic Advisory Council and an eminent panel of Honorary Fellows. Together with other academics, they review prospective IEA publications, their comments being passed on anonymously to authors. All IEA papers are therefore subject to the same rigorous independent refereeing process as used by leading academic journals.

IEA publications enjoy widespread classroom use and course adoptions in schools and universities. They are also sold throughout the world and often translated/reprinted.

Since 1974 the IEA has helped to create a worldwide network of 100 similar institutions in over 70 countries. They are all independent but share the IEA's mission.

Views expressed in the IEA's publications are those of the authors, not those of the Institute (which has no corporate view), its Managing Trustees, Academic Advisory Council members or senior staff.

Members of the Institute's Academic Advisory Council, Honorary Fellows, Trustees and Staff are listed on the following page.

The Institute gratefully acknowledges financial support for its publications programme and other work from a generous benefaction by the late Alec and Beryl Warren.

Other papers recently published by the IEA include:

Economy and Virtue
Essays on the Theme of Markets and Morality
Edited by Dennis O'Keeffe
Readings 59; ISBN 0 255 36504 7; £12.50

Free Markets Under Siege
Cartels, Politics and Social Welfare
Richard A. Epstein
Occasional Paper 132; ISBN 0 255 36553 5; £10.00

Unshackling Accountants
D. R. Myddelton
Hobart Paper 149; ISBN 0 255 36559 4; £12.50

The Euro as Politics
Pedro Schwartz
Research Monograph 58; ISBN 0 255 36535 7; £12.50

Pricing Our Roads
Vision and Reality
Stephen Glaister & Daniel J. Graham
Research Monograph 59; ISBN 0 255 36562 4; £10.00

The Role of Business in the Modern World
Progress, Pressures, and Prospects for the Market Economy
David Henderson
Hobart Paper 150; ISBN 0 255 36548 9; £12.50

Public Service Broadcasting Without the BBC?
Alan Peacock
Occasional Paper 133; ISBN 0 255 36565 9; £10.00

The ECB and the Euro: the First Five Years
Otmar Issing
Occasional Paper 134; ISBN 0 255 36555 1; £10.00

Towards a Liberal Utopia?
Edited by Philip Booth
Hobart Paperback 32; ISBN 0 255 36563 2; £15.00

The Way Out of the Pensions Quagmire
Philip Booth & Deborah Cooper
Research Monograph 60; ISBN 0 255 36517 9; £12.50

Black Wednesday
A Re-examination of Britain's Experience in the Exchange Rate Mechanism
Alan Budd
Occasional Paper 135; ISBN 0 255 36566 7; £7.50

Crime: Economic Incentives and Social Networks
Paul Ormerod
Hobart Paper 151; ISBN 0 255 36554 3; £10.00

The Road to Serfdom *with* **The Intellectuals and Socialism**
Friedrich A. Hayek
Occasional Paper 136; ISBN 0 255 36576 4; £10.00

Money and Asset Prices in Boom and Bust
Tim Congdon
Hobart Paper 152; ISBN 0 255 36570 5; £10.00

The Dangers of Bus Re-regulation
and Other Perspectives on Markets in Transport
John Hibbs et al.
Occasional Paper 137; ISBN 0 255 36572 1; £10.00

The New Rural Economy
Change, Dynamism and Government Policy
Berkeley Hill et al.
Occasional Paper 138; ISBN 0 255 36546 2; £15.00

The Benefits of Tax Competition
Richard Teather
Hobart Paper 153; ISBN 0 255 36569 1; £12.50

Wheels of Fortune
Self-funding Infrastructure and the Free Market Case for a Land Tax
Fred Harrison
Hobart Paper 154; ISBN 0 255 36589 6; £12.50

Were 364 Economists All Wrong?
Edited by Philip Booth
Readings 60; ISBN 978 0 255 36588 8; £10.00

Europe After the 'No' Votes
Mapping a New Economic Path
Patrick A. Messerlin
Occasional Paper 139; ISBN 978 0 255 36580 2; £10.00

The Railways, the Market and the Government
John Hibbs et al.
Readings 61; ISBN 978 0 255 36567 3; £12.50

Corruption: The World's Big C
Cases, Causes, Consequences, Cures
Ian Senior
Research Monograph 61; ISBN 978 0 255 36571 0; £12.50

Choice and the End of Social Housing
Peter King
Hobart Paper 155; ISBN 978 0 255 36568 0; £10.00

Sir Humphrey's Legacy
Facing Up to the Cost of Public Sector Pensions
Neil Record
Hobart Paper 156; ISBN 978 0 255 36578 9; £10.00

The Economics of Law
Cento Veljanovski
Second edition
Hobart Paper 157; ISBN 978 0 255 36561 1; £12.50

They Meant Well
Government Project Disasters
D. R. Myddelton
Hobart Paper 160; ISBN 978 0 255 36601 4; £12.50

Rescuing Social Capital from Social Democracy
John Meadowcroft & Mark Pennington
Hobart Paper 161; ISBN 978 0 255 36592 5; £10.00

Paths to Property
Approaches to Institutional Change in International Development
Karol Boudreaux & Paul Dragos Aligica
Hobart Paper 162; ISBN 978 0 255 36582 6; £10.00

Prohibitions
Edited by John Meadowcroft
Hobart Paperback 35; ISBN 978 0 255 36585 7; £15.00

Trade Policy, New Century
The WTO, FTAs and Asia Rising
Razeen Sally
Hobart Paper 163; ISBN 978 0 255 36544 4; £12.50

Sixty Years On – Who Cares for the NHS?
Helen Evans
Research Monograph 63; ISBN 978 0 255 36611 3; £10.00

Taming Leviathan
Waging the War of Ideas Around the World
Edited by Colleen Dyble
Occasional Paper 142; ISBN 978 0 255 36607 6; £12.50

The Legal Foundations of Free Markets
Edited by Stephen F. Copp
Hobart Paperback 36; ISBN 978 0 255 36591 8; £15.00

Climate Change Policy: Challenging the Activists
Edited by Colin Robinson
Readings 62; ISBN 978 0 255 36595 6; £10.00

Should We Mind the Gap?
Gender Pay Differentials and Public Policy
J. R. Shackleton
Hobart Paper 164; ISBN 978 0 255 36604 5; £10.00

Pension Provision: Government Failure Around the World
Edited by Philip Booth et al.
Readings 63; ISBN 978 0 255 36602 1; £15.00

New Europe's Old Regions
Piotr Zientara
Hobart Paper 165; ISBN 978 0 255 36617 5; £12.50

Central Banking in a Free Society
Tim Congdon
Hobart Paper 166; ISBN 978 0 255 36623 6; £12.50

Verdict on the Crash: Causes and Policy Implications
Edited by Philip Booth
Hobart Paperback 37; ISBN 978 0 255 36635 9; £12.50

Other IEA publications

Comprehensive information on other publications and the wider work
of the IEA can be found at www.iea.org.uk. To order any publication
please see below.

Personal customers

Orders from personal customers should be directed to the IEA:
Bob Layson
IEA
2 Lord North Street
FREEPOST LON10168
London SW1P 3YZ
Tel: 020 7799 8909. Fax: 020 7799 2137
Email: blayson@iea.org.uk

Trade customers

All orders from the book trade should be directed to the IEA's
distributor:
Gazelle Book Services Ltd (IEA Orders)
FREEPOST RLYS-EAHU-YSCZ
White Cross Mills
Hightown
Lancaster LA1 4XS
Tel: 01524 68765, Fax: 01524 53232
Email: sales@gazellebooks.co.uk

IEA subscriptions

The IEA also offers a subscription service to its publications. For a single
annual payment (currently £42.00 in the UK), subscribers receive every
monograph the IEA publishes. For more information please contact:
Adam Myers
Subscriptions
IEA
2 Lord North Street
FREEPOST LON10168
London SW1P 3YZ
Tel: 020 7799 8920, Fax: 020 7799 2137
Email: amyers@iea.org.uk